REVERSE PSYCHOLOGY MARKETING

REVERSE PSYCHOLOGY MARKETING

The Death of Traditional Marketing and the Rise of the New "Pull" Game

Indrajit Sinha
Thomas Foscht

First published 2007 by
PALGRAVE MACMILLAN
Houndmills, Basingstoke, Hampshire RG21 6XS and
175 Fifth Avenue, New York, N.Y. 10010
Companies and representatives throughout the world

PALGRAVE MACMILLAN is the global academic imprint of the Palgrave
Macmillan division of St. Martin's Press, LLC and of Palgrave Macmillan Ltd.
Macmillan® is a registered trademark in the United States, United Kingdom
and other countries. Palgrave is a registered trademark in the European
Union and other countries.

ISBN-13: 978–0–230–50754–8
ISBN-10: 0–230–50754–9

This book is printed on paper suitable for recycling and made from fully
managed and sustained forest sources.

A catalogue record for this book is available from the British Library.

A catalog record for this book is available from the Library of Congress.

10   9   8   7   6   5   4   3   2   1
16 15 14 13 12 11 10 09 08 07

Printed and bound in China

*For my parents, Mr Justice (Retd) Sujit K. Sinha
and Mrs Lina Sinha*

– I.S.

*For my parents, Mr Maximilian Foscht and
Mrs Christine Foscht*

– T.F.

Contents

Prologue

Right in the heart of New York's Manhattan, in a busy shopping area, is a nondescript "store". It has no exterior signs, no billboards, no inviting posters on the windows – indeed nothing that would identify it as a regular shop. Yet curious onlookers and itinerant tourists usually amble into it, seduced perhaps by the sight of tastefully bedecked mannequins that are clearly visible through its large French windows. Some of them think that it is perhaps a designer's atelier or studio, or perhaps even an *avant-garde* dress gallery. But once inside, there is no mistaking that it is like any other upscale apparel shop with racks of clothing all bearing price tags. A bemused enquiry to an assistant elicits a discreet response: "This is a Prada store."

Those who practice marketing for a living and anyone even remotely associated with business will tell you that marketing is all about creating a favorable perception and about getting publicity, the more the better. The key lies in a word called "differentiation". It is the way of separating one's own offering from one's rivals, pointing out of the pros of the former and the cons of the latter. A clever student of a marketing course at any of the worldwide business schools quickly picks up the axioms that are embedded in the so-called "marketing bibles": "Love the customer, not the product"; "Use segmentation to target the customer"; "Understand customer needs"; "Mass customization is the future"; "Promotions result in more sales"; and so on. Indeed, these notions are so pervasive that one does not need to have been in a business school to be able to use them intelligently. When we told our friends that we were writing a business book for practitioners with some new ideas in it, many offered helpful tips and advice: "Get a review from Amazon"; "Send a copy to Oprah"; "Get endorsements from Porter, Peters, Prahalad, Kotler"; . . . and such heavy-weight business gurus.

Yet, as the above Prada example shows, things are changing in business and society, often imperceptibly and without much fanfare. Shops for teenagers in Tokyo's *chic* Harajuku district also go without signs, the idea being that if you do not know it is a shop, you have no business being there. In a marked departure from previous Olympic games, the organizers of the Athens Olympics *actually* sought to minimize commercial displays. The CEO of Ryanair tells complaining customers to take a hike (albeit, more descriptively) and not to bother him, since he is doing all he can by giving such extraordinarily low fares. Mass-market products like jeans and sneakers are now advertised with the explicit message that they, like Ferraris, are *not* meant for everybody. The co-CEO of Hermès, the super-exclusive French luxury label, openly says to a newspaper that his job is *not* to understand customers. Instead of listening to customers' likes and dislikes, firms now dictate what customers should have – in a way that is more reminiscent of the Soup Nazi in the classic *Seinfeld* episode. And rather like a middle-school matron, Wal-Mart and Tesco, two of the world's largest retailers, screen their music CDs and DVDs for "objectionable" material and peremptorily refuse to carry those that fail their tests.

We, as two marketing professors, one based in the U.S. and the other in Europe, have not failed to notice this singular development in the last few years. Traditional marketing is now being turned on its head, as a result of both a popular backlash against traditional business norms and practices and the actions of a few pioneering firms, who, either by design or accident, have caught on to the trend. Influential cost-conscious companies like Wal-Mart, Ryanair, and Tesco have also unwittingly fed the movement, though with unintended and not entirely desirable consequences. Reverse psychology marketing, pull marketing, and anti-marketing are not buzzwords yet, but perspicacious marketers and sociologists must have realized that some deep and unmistakable change is afoot in the global culture. An online audience in Russia recently chose a "plain and natural-looking" schoolgirl in a beauty contest over more conventional beauties. More than 40,000 Russians voted for her under the slogan "Say No to Barbie Dolls".

This book is about that change.

Notes on authors

Dr Indrajit "Jay" Sinha is Washburn Research Fellow and Associate Professor of Marketing in the Fox School of Business & Management of Temple University, Philadelphia, USA. He holds a Bachelor's degree in Computer Science & Engineering, two Master's degrees in Management and Statistics, and a PhD in Business Administration earned from the University of Michigan, Ann Arbor. He has also worked in the management consulting practice of Deloitte & Touche. He has an active research agenda focusing on the meaning and symbolism of brands in contemporary society, and their role in the age of globalization, the Internet, and mobile telecommunications. His articles have appeared in several prestigious marketing and strategy journals. His *Harvard Business Review* article on branding and cost transparency was highlighted in op-ed columns in the *The Sunday Times* of London and the *Industry Standard*, and has been used as required reading at business schools worldwide. He is frequently interviewed by the national and international media. He has offered courses and workshops at the Columbia Business School, ESCP-EAP (Paris), Temple University (Japan), and the Hong Kong University of Science & Technology. He lives in Philadelphia. He may be reached at isinha@temple.edu.

Dr Thomas Foscht is Associate Professor of Marketing at the Department of Marketing and Retailing in the University of Graz, Austria, where he received his MBA and PhD in Business Administration degrees. He also holds a diploma in Mechanical Engineering. He presently serves as the Vice Chairman of the department, as Co-Director of the EMBA-program, and as a referee for the Austrian Court. His research areas are marketing management, customer relationship management, consumer behavior, and international marketing. He has authored several managerial articles, monographs, and books on customer loyalty and marketing strategy. His textbook on buyer behavior is widely used in the German-speaking countries. He is regularly interviewed by the European media and has consulted to leading Austrian and German firms. He has given courses and lectures in many universities of Europe, the U.S., and Asia. He lives in Graz. He may be reached at thomas.foscht@uni-graz.at.

1

Death knell for traditional marketing

How the mighty have fallen! Only a decade ago, many a business observer would have been hard-pressed to think that there would come a day when Pepsi would become more valuable than the venerable Coca-Cola company, that pesky newcomers like Southwest Airlines and Ryanair would outperform flagship national carriers, that Tesco would upstage the grande-dame of British retailing Marks & Spencer, or that a global upstart like Samsung would dwarf the archetype of "made in Japan" prestige – Sony. And that people would one day be speculating about the imminent demise of Ford and General Motors.

Let us make a disclaimer right upfront. This book is not about engaging in the familiar blame-and-praise game for the so-called "losers" and "winners" of the current business environment. It does not seek to cite examples *du jour* only to extricate from them a certain tenuous insight that may be valid today yet fail tomorrow. Indeed, one can certainly expect the tables to be turned – that Coke will make a triumphant comeback from the ailing situation it finds itself in or that Sony will revive its fortunes under its new chief. But we mention the above headlines in order to make a point. We strongly believe that many of the firms that are in trouble today and those that have failed recently have done so because they have been ill-served by their own *marketing*. This has happened to their managers unwittingly and despite their best interests. Something deeper and more substantial is afoot in business today, which is changing the familiar script of marketing. The game is different now – one that strays from the prescriptions that traditional marketing theory holds dear, indeed that sometimes works in a way that is counter to it (what we call "anti-marketing") and that lays focus on network-building and "pulling the customer" above all else. Many experienced hands in corporate boardrooms are oblivious to these shifting sands and evolving trends, and are paying the price as a result.

Revolutionary may sound sensational and catchy, but what is happening these days is not far from that. We are living at a time when stores exist without sign-boards, thriving instead on a fertile youth grapevine network; when chefs insist that their rich clientèle can *only* select from a limited menu chosen for that day; when officially "slow cities" proudly embrace a relaxed pace and disallow fast-food and franchise establishments within their limits; and when advertisements that once had glamorous models now show

very real people with all of their imperfections –
warts, paunches, freckles, *et al.*

Firms that are wedded to playing the old game are
now being handily outfoxed by their more nimble
rivals, who have their ears closer to the ground.
Coca-Cola still remains committed to the idea of
furnishing the world with Coke, believing that traditional marketing is the panacea and that nostalgic
and sentimental Coke ads will regain the favors of
its worldwide fan-base. In his inauguration speech,
Neville Isdell, the latest in a succession of recent
Coca-Cola CEOs, reaffirmed his goal to make the
flagship Coke brand great again. Perhaps, to say otherwise in the staunchly rigid culture of his Atlanta
headquarters would have been blasphemous, but the
fact remains that traditional soft drinks are a dying
breed. Pepsi understands better the reality of moms
from Moscow to Mumbai who now consciously
avoid buying carbonated drinks for their kids prefer-
ring instead bottled water and juices. And that for
an increasing number of people up-market mineral
water is the "new wine", supplanting the latter on
lunch and dinner tables in haute-cuisine restaurants.
Accordingly, Pepsi has diversified its product port-
folio to reflect those trends while Coke continues
to aggressively market its soda brands, hoping that
somehow the Mexican math (i.e., the highest per-
capita consumption) will catch on in the rest of the
populous world, particularly in China and India.

Consider the story of Sony and Samsung – the new Sony. The former, an iconic global brand, had gradually built its market dominance from the 1960s onward by introducing a series of sleek, well-designed, and market-friendly products – transistor radios, televisions, and Walkmans. Innovation was only a sub-text for these early Sony gadgets. Indeed, some of them were hardly innovative at all, like the transistor radio, which was invented in America, and the Walkman, which was only a portable cassette player. But, Sony's *forte* was the design of its products – smaller than its rival brands, clever, and appealing. In the early years, buying a Sony product was not beyond the reach of the average buyer. Indeed, as co-founder Akio Morita wrote in his autobiography, the company went to great lengths to reduce the manufacturing cost in order to make its items accessible to the average Japanese. Besides, it was the low-paid rank and file American GIs that had given Sony its reputation in the West as a large number of them had brought its pocket transistors back from Japan.

But, somehow along the way, during the late 1980s and 1990s, Sony lost the script and the recipe that had contributed to its success. It began to believe in its own marketing and catchphrases – as the purveyor of the most innovative gadgets and games. Its managers became fixated on this brand image and innovation became an end in itself. Accordingly, Sony sought to introduce the most advanced Playstation, the most amazing Aibo robot, the sleekest

Vaio laptop, and Cybershot camera – all of which predictably courted the affluent buyer. The tagline "It's a Sony" underlined the special nature of the purchase and that the Sony product was superior to the rest, which justified the higher price. Indeed, Sony products soon became a luxury purchase for the average buyer, who despite wanting to get one could not afford the price margin just for the sake of a better design. In the developing countries, middle-class shoppers began to avoid Sony showrooms altogether since their salespeople did not give discounts and deals as the Korean companies did. Sony effectively became a "prisoner of its marketing", confined in an ivory tower of its own making.

Samsung, formerly a stodgy and geriatric Korean *chaebol*, had undergone a transformation of its own during the Asian recession years of the late 1990s. It recruited a team of young and dynamic managers, who regarded Sony as an ideal exemplar and carefully charted the factors that had initially led to Sony's popularity. They wanted to emulate the sleek designs in their products, but instead of crafting a fancy, eye-catching brand campaign like the later Sony, they focused on developing a core *network* of buyers first. Whereas Sony would not (or could not) come down from its lofty price perch, Samsung frequently would and did. That generated the so-called "wow factor" among the growing number of young Samsung enthusiasts. They raved over the nice-looking mobile flip-phones with in-built camera and lots of features, yet at prices that seemed reasonable.

As they talked to their parents and friends, the network grew in a gradual snowballing effect and at a sustained pace. The goodwill that Samsung had engendered with their mobile phones soon carried over to its other more profitable electronic items. Now, shoppers were increasingly willing to try out the Samsung brand for more expensive items like flat screen televisions. Samsung's focus on network over marketing had paid off.

How and why marketing is metamorphosing

Surprisingly or not, as one's viewpoint may be, academics who teach marketing for a living and professionals who practice it in the field have not grasped the true nature, scope, and impact of the changes that have surreptitiously come over their discipline. Everyone senses that things are going to be different from the diminishing numbers of mainstream media audiences compared with the massive popularity of Internet websites and blogs (online diaries). One frequently sees such headlines as "the death of advertising" but the impact on marketing itself is not widely debated or questioned. Millions around the world now write these blogs with journalistic dedication and are avidly read by many more. This understandably makes marketing managers sit up and take notice, but the ideas of how to best make use of them to sell products follow a predictable script. One hears that a certain car company executive maintains his own blog and that companies ought to encourage employees to insert favorable mentions about new offerings. But to apply these tired old tactics in the newly created realm of blogosphere is not just doomed to failure but may even be counterproductive. Bloggers, who have the same distrust of business as an average WTO protestor, will shame the offending firm through endless ridicule at their unseemly desperation to hawk their wares. Marketers need to be savvier and have to think and act like the bloggers themselves. For a start, and as we detail later, they would do well to understand how the dynamics of customer networks operate and who and what influence clusters of people positively and negatively.

There is now a growing impression among senior managers and entrepreneurs that traditional "push marketing" – as laid down by the "bibles" that an MBA student learns at a business school – no longer addresses the expediencies of today's marketplace. The chief marketing officer of American Express John Hayes says publicly, "With the way the consumer is behaving today in *all* markets, more and more you have to create a *pull* dynamic" (italics added for emphasis). More than a few uneasy murmurs are routinely heard in corporate boardrooms about the *visible* return on the marketing dollar. Indeed, after two decades of heavy spending on advertising, branding, product launches, and promotions, many multinational companies seem weary and uncertain about marketing, its role and effect today, and are cautiously feeling out how the winds have shifted. Some firms, particularly those whose market shares have been slipping or which are facing painful cost pressure from Asian-based competitors, have drastically scaled back their marketing budgets altogether.

On the other hand, successful business owners are now heard taking pride in how *little* they spend on marketing and how they are changing the rules by practicing reverse psychology tactics. Indeed, a few like the super-exclusive Aman Resorts and the cult apparel brand, A Bathing Ape (BAPE, for short) shun publicity altogether, content to operate below the gaze of popular media and culture, and manage to thrive just the same. University Sportswear, a fast expanding youth-apparel retailer in American malls, has been growing virtually by word-of-mouth alone since it practically spends next to nothing on advertising. The company is defying an age-old industry norm of heavy spending on marketing and brand awareness building. IndiOne, a successful ultra-cheap hotel in the Indian tech-hub Bangalore, employs only seven full-time employees, does no advertising and promotions, and boasts of an operating margin as high as 65 percent, which could be the envy of any major hotel-chain. There is a new crop of up-market restaurants and nightclubs turning up each year in every metropolis that rent space in a nondescript high-rise or a marginal neighborhood and adopt a policy of no advertising and no overt signage. Red Bull, the popular Austrian energy

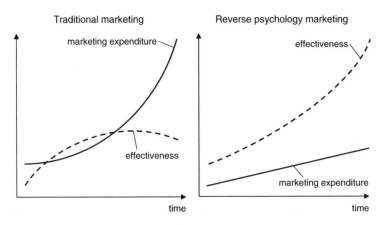

Figure 1.1   Comparison of expenditure and effectiveness

drink, limits traditional advertising in favor of sponsorships of the so-called "extreme sports", F1 racing, and other events that appeal to the global youth.

Figure 1.1 illustrates the contrasting effectiveness and returns from pursuing the two kinds of marketing. Traditional marketing costs more and shows a distinct saturation effect, becoming progressively less effective beyond a certain point. This happens despite the best efforts of managers, as consumer boredom and resentment set in and people show a stark aversion to being constantly told by marketers what to do. In contrast, reverse psychology marketing tactics are considerably more effective, costing much less and providing significantly higher returns. Not surprisingly, more and more firms are opting to follow the latter scheme.

The above pattern is not limited to the niche, youth-oriented, or high-priced categories. The marketing that mass-market firms have been doing lately has also tended to become understated, cost-driven, and minimalist. Discounters like Wal-Mart, Lidl, Ryanair, Southwest, and Ikea call attention to the bargain prices they offer and how they are therefore working on behalf of their customers. But customer service, once considered the hallmark of good marketing, is becoming increasingly non-existent at many of these places. Even mainstream firms are not exempt from these winds of change. More and more stores expect shoppers to bag their own purchases, companies increasingly encourage their clients to self-serve themselves on the Internet, and airlines in the U.S. and Europe even charge for on-board meals. A joke in Europe ran that the customer service department at Ryanair consists of two people, till the company pointed out it actually employs *around twenty*.

Yet, marketing, in its influence and consequences, remains just as important today as it did before. While large American and European corporations have been shedding business functions, like accounting, employee management, and information technology, wholesale and delegating them to business process outsourcing (BPO) entities in India and elsewhere, everyone realizes marketing is too critical an operation to be outsourced or left in the hands of consultants. The idea of remaining close (physically, if not metaphorically) to one's customer does not seem in danger of being considered obsolete – at least not yet. Marketing, when viewed as the "art of selling", not only brings home the bacon, but more fundamentally, since it creates a brand, it is the "face" of business itself. It is that vital bridge function that links the boundaries of a business with society as a whole. Therefore, in this age of outsourcing and offshoring, when the entire business appears to have come unhinged, when Chinese sub-contractors manufacture the goods and Indian BPO agencies manage accounting, payroll, and customer relations, Western companies find that they have been reduced to the most elemental of business operations – getting customers and keeping them.

While that basic role of marketing still remains paramount, the fact remains that the rules of the marketing game have changed. Part of the reason has to do with the aforementioned transformation of business itself, what is considered essential and what can be let out to others. The relentless pressure to reduce costs that now weighs heavily on nearly all companies also causes them to rethink what *kind* of marketing is best suited to their needs. Some have decided to forgo traditional advertising practices altogether, finding them to be ineffectual luxuries. Technology is partly another reason as it encroaches ever so gradually into the familiar domains that marketing once considered its own. In the old days, the marketing manager oversaw the ranks of the sales force and customer service representatives. Now, specialized software, for example, sales force automation (SFA) and customer relationship management (CRM), has co-opted many of the manager's former functions. Technology has even managed to apportion the tasks

that a paid employee once performed to an average customer, which gives the latter a healthy sense
of control and empowerment. For instance, online
banking is allowing clients to conduct their everyday
business: check balances, pay bills, and seamlessly
move money across accounts, resulting in substantial
cost efficiencies for individual banks.

Perhaps, the most important reason why the old
marketing game no longer holds true today is that
the broader environment itself has changed. Modern
society is unrecognizable from the 1950s and 1960s
when the theories and precepts of traditional marketing came into being. Ideas such as the marketing
concept, marketing mix (4 Ps), customer segmentation, product positioning, and strategies and tactics
in pricing and promotions were developed in a relatively static society, where the social hierarchy was
largely based on class and income, and consumption
patterns were relatively stable and predictable. General Motors could easily range its car models from
Chevrolet on one end to Cadillac on the other to
match the buying power of Americans and this was
a simple, foolproof recipe for success. Back then, the
consumer was fresh and impressionable, who could
be easily swayed by the images and sounds coming
from a television set into thinking that a new product
could magically alter her life. Today's consumer is a
strange species whose buying behavior could seem as
an unfathomable mystery even to the best marketing
expert. He or she is the prototypical *hybrid* shopper who defies the purchasing logic from any social

class-, income- or education-based model. She may buy an expensive Louis Vuitton bag to match her inexpensive H&M dress and drive to a Target store in her Mercedes. (A Mercedes-Benz ad in America actually shows a woman delivering newspapers in a fashionable neighborhood from her new C-Class.) All through this modern consumer's high-school and college, she has likely been fed on a diet of books and articles from anti-business and anti-globalization authors like Naomi Klein and Arundhati Roy. She is therefore blasé, cynical, and distrustful of business in general and advertising in particular. The mobile phone and the Internet are inseparable parts of her being and she is able to communicate with friends and receive and disseminate information in ways so powerful and dramatic that marketing scientists do not fully understand.

It should not seem such a surprise then that traditional marketing is out of step with the present time. Unlike economics, accounting, and finance whose principles and axioms are relatively stable and immutable, those of marketing are inextricably tied to and aligned with the broader business and social environments, which are in turn volatile and dynamic. Increasingly, therefore, those companies that are playing by the traditional rules and pushing more of the same old ideas on their ever-disgruntled customers are losing out and are seeing their once-mighty brands diluted and watered down to the point of irrelevance. In the next chapter, we consider how such over-marketing tactics proved to be the bane of many firms that were once considered giants and icons in their respective countries. In contrast, savvier players like Samsung, Red Bull, Tchibo, Southwest, Whole Foods, Wal-Mart, and Lidl, which have better understood the new game, have done well as a result.

So, what are the rules of this new marketing game? We have found that (refer to Table 1.1):

Table 1.1   Marketing's metamorphosis

	Old Game	**New Game**
Central Focus	Customer	Product, Cost→Brand
Objective	Profit	Network→Profit
Marketing Mix	4 Ps (price, product, place, promotion)	3 Bs (brand, buyer network, buying or supply chain)
Segment Structure	Discount, Standard, Premium	Hard Discount, Ultra Premium
Brand Differentiator	Quality	Design
Supply (or Buying) Chain	Subsumed under Channel strategy, Modest emphasis	Independent key to the Business Model, Absolutely vital for firm success
Network Building Model	Directive, Firm at center	Buzz or Viral, built around "Hubs"
Advertising message	Superiority claims, Unique Selling Propositions (USPs), Use of Glamour, Humor, Irony, etc. to sell the firm and the product	Counter-intuitive, Brutally honest, Real people, Deflecting attention from the firm, Zen (minimalist and understated)

1. The customer is no longer the *central* focus of firms' decisions. Instead, firms have chosen to adhere strongly to a product and cost imperative. This may sound like a radical departure from traditional marketing, but it is solidly grounded in the reality of the present. Indeed, when one considers the pitfalls and crevices that many firms have mired themselves in while attempting to pursue the fickle whims of customers, it does not seem such a major pragmatic leap after all. We discuss this further in Chapter 2.

2. The strategic objective of a firm is now to build and sustain a viable customer network by drawing from its product and cost advantages. Profits are a byproduct of this framework, and they will readily follow if the firm executes the core network objective (discussed in more detail in Chapter 4).

3. The time has come to shelve the so-called "4 Ps" of the marketing mix. Instead, marketers are better off thinking their strategy in terms of 3 Bs (brand, buyer network, and buying chain). More on this is given below.

4. The traditional three-tier market structure (discount, standard, and premium segments) is quickly disappearing. Instead, the middle market is caving in and industries are getting splintered into *only* the hard discount and ultra-premium segments – metaphorically like Wal-Marts and Ferraris (discussed in Chapter 3).

5. In most product categories, quality has plateaued to such an extent that most consumers consider

it as a given and therefore not a discriminator in their choice decisions. Instead, the *design* of the brand has become the new differentiator (discussed in Chapter 5).

6. In the traditional marketing model the discussion of buying (or supply) chain fell under the place or channel criterion. Its importance was not independently highlighted in the marketing mix program. At the present time, supply-chain is widely considered to be the crux of the entire business itself whose importance cannot be overstated. Indeed, it has become the ultimate determinant of a business model's efficacy. As we discuss below, competition among firms is effectively now a "beauty contest" of their respective supply-chains.

7. The traditional directive promotion model, where the firm saw its role as a consumer's educator and transmitted its messages via advertising and other means to an external audience, is becoming increasingly obsolete. Instead, the new model emphasizes the influence of a customer network where the firm does not have an overt role. Instead, one or more "hubs" (opinion leaders, celebrities, brand ambassadors, etc.) act as the disseminators of the buzz (discussed in Chapter 4).

8. Finally, the age-old premises of advertising body-copy, that of showing the firm in a more favorable light than its competitors, making superiority claims to attract attention, and so

on, are losing ground today. What works in advertising now is the counter-intuitive, brutally honest, unpretentious, and understated message. A number of creative firms have engaged in novel anti-marketing tactics (discussed in Chapter 6), which seem to be more in tune with today's society and culture, and are therefore more effective.

Shifting focus from the customer to cost

A realization is dawning upon most businesses that not all customers are created equal, and the firm is better off staying true to its inner mission and in not over-catering to attract fickle buyers, who will depart at the first sight of a better deal. Consequently, the new breed of firms that are now the shining success stories in their countries all execute from a common script. They have made it their singular mission to focus on costs like a laser beam, believing that in the end that is what their customers truly want. Their motto therefore is "Lower costs and they'll come."

Wal-Mart, Tesco, Aldi, Lidl, Ryanair, Southwest, Ikea, and Schlecker (Europe's number one drug-store) each pay lip-service to acting on behalf of their customers, but their true calling is to drive their entire organization toward a ferocious cost battle. Hence, these businesses attempt to please customers *indirectly* at the checkout aisle by affording them greater savings, but not from providing better customer service. Ryanair's chairman Michael O'Leary reportedly told off a customer who had complained to him about bad service by saying that he is doing all he can by lowering airfares each day. The airline now charges its passengers an extra fee for checked-in baggage. The vast majority of Ryanair clients, who benefit from truly rock-bottom fares on convenient connections, do not appear to have a problem with such a philosophy. The popular German discounter Lidl likewise avoids what it calls unnecessary frills on presentation and store layout, selling items directly from the supplier boxes and pallets with the catchy slogan "At Lidl we keep everything simple, that's why you save more."

We should note at this point that while it is understandable why these firms have focused on reducing cost (namely, to steal a march over their rivals), it is neither desirable nor effective to lower service below that threshold level that customers have come to *expect*. Buyers are willing to give up on certain rights and privileges in return for a bargain price, but only to a point. Too much downgrading of either the product or the service in the interest of costs could lead to widespread customer resentment, which a savvy competitor can easily exploit. In America, the Target chain has succeeded in playing up its trendier offerings and better service vis-à-vis Wal-Mart while remaining competitive on price.

If the above examples seem somewhat extreme or perhaps representing only the hard discount segment, the same idea of firms no longer placing the customer on the pedestal can be seen in the higher and more mainstream market tiers as well. American passengers are now used to paying for their food, beverages, and headsets on their cost-strapped airlines. Stores in the U.S. that once had the most liberal merchandise return policies in the world have clamped down considerably. Some British banks reportedly route customer calls to an automated line versus a human agent depending on a computer program that determines the customer's perceived value to the firm. Finally, in the luxury segment the focus is not on customer or cost but on the delivery of a truly superior product. The co-CEO of Hermès, the ultra-luxury French label, is heard telling a *Financial Times* reporter that his company does not commission market studies or conduct focus groups like other companies. In fact, he says, *"we're not trying to understand what the customer wants*, but to bring our customers into our world, to convince them via the product" (italics added). Obviously, a major sea-change has taken place in business when the chairman of a top-notch brand admits publicly that he doesn't adhere to that bedrock axiom of traditional marketing, that of listening to customers. This is where the new game takes off.

Time to shelve the 4 Ps

Finally, it is becoming increasingly obvious that the so-called "4 Ps" (product, price, place, and promotion) of the marketing mix program have become outdated and ineffectual to address the complexities of modern business. When this idea was mooted in America in the 1950s, marketing, like the society it was operating in, was a relatively straightforward affair. Managers needed to articulate these four aspects of their marketing plan rather like choices from a set menu and their job was basically done. Over time the 4 Ps became such an article of faith in marketing that no self-respecting strategic plan could be considered complete without it.

As we have alluded to earlier, we are now living in an era of outsourcing, when the product strategy has either devolved completely from the business or is developed in conjunction with the sub-contracting firms. The latter like Flextronics, Quanta, Solectron, and Celestica are highly sophisticated electronic manufacturing services (EMS) operations that regularly come up with a product strategy of their own for many of their multinational clients and have the wherewithal to develop proprietary designs for rival firms even within the same industry. Singapore-based Flextronics, which has some 90 plants in 30 countries, is now one of the world's biggest suppliers of mobile phones and consumers electronics. It also makes printers for HP and Epson, X-Box consoles for Microsoft, copiers for Xerox, PDAs for Casio, and so on. The contribution of these contract manufacturers is truly a hidden secret of today's global economy.

Even in those cases where the firm has total and undivided control over its product strategy and the product is the sum total of its business (as for a technology or luxury firm), it is in the end an input to how well it is able to execute the *brand* concept. The 4 Ps idea is mute on the critical subject of branding, which we discuss in-depth in the next chapter. In fact, the principal problem with the 4 Ps thinking is that it presupposes that these four aspects are somehow independent decisions for the individual firm. But, in reality, all of these decisions are intrinsically and overtly interrelated under the brand umbrella. When the firm conceives of its offering in terms of a brand, it is better able to conceptualize how the product will mesh with an appropriate price point, distribution plan, and promotion tactic. The Austrian energy drink Red Bull, which is presently a youth phenomenon and therefore a favorite case study among consultants and business school professors, offers an interesting viewpoint. Red Bull sells a product it cannot legally patent, since such energy drinks have long existed in various Asian countries, like Thailand and Japan. Its entire business hence revolves around selling the brand to young people. This the company does by not following the script of traditional marketing but from various non-traditional, network-building means, such as "seeding the brand" through disc jockeys, bartenders, college students, and F1 car racing.

The Red Bull example brings us to the second problem of the 4 Ps approach. It effectively assumes the firm's customers to be passive, somewhat hapless entities, whom the marketing mix will readily convert into willing buyers. Indeed, the 4 Ps seem to exist insulated from the world of buyers. While this may have worked during the early marketing years, firms increasingly have to seek out subtler and more refined ways of selling at the present time. In the rest of this book, we describe various novel and counter-intuitive reverse psychology tactics that are currently being practiced to develop and sustain a customer network.

Lastly, the 4 Ps concept is also silent on arguably the most important element of a firm's marketing program today: its supply chain. It is often said, with a lot of truth, that competition across firms these days is effectively a beauty contest of their respective supply chains. The reason Wal-Mart, Dell, Ikea, and Tesco are able to handily outwit their rivals lies squarely in the way each has systematically built up its supply chain over time, by rigorously screening suppliers, making them outbid and compete with each other, and by modernizing the whole process with the latest technology. Indeed, no marketing strategy would be complete today without articulating a functional, viable, and cost-effective supply chain. Thus, to sum up, the firm is far better off conceiving and developing its programs not from 4 Ps but from 3 Bs instead: brand, buyer network, and buying (or supply-) chain.

Let us now look deeper into these and other aspects of this new marketing game.

2

Over-marketing and brand suicide

Switch on your computer's broadband Internet connection and you are instantaneously bombarded with a blizzard of pop-up ads, all trying to sell you something. Marketers now call you at home, load your message inbox with annoying junk mail, and then not so discreetly "place" their products within movies and television shows. The rationale they offer is that they are new ways of selling. Yet, are these intrusive and unsubtle techniques at all effective? In our view, any short-term gains that these ploys achieve by luring a few incidental buyers are overwhelmingly defeated by the longer-term damage to the brands, which is far more pernicious. In fact, these are the ways push marketers are engaging in a collective hara-kiri through cheapening their brand value. To understand how and why this is taking place, let us take a short detour into the intriguing world of branding and brands.

Since the mid-1980s, the meanings, symbolism, strengths, and potentialities of a brand have variously intrigued, fascinated, befuddled, and stymied the imaginations of many a marketing and strategy practitioner. In its most basic sense of course, a brand implies an *instance* of a product or service category just as an Adidas sneaker, Xerox copier, and Google search engine. But to take this literal textbook definition is to belittle the enormous outlay of energy, time, and money that firms expend in creating and managing the visible icons of business, like the swoosh that replaces Nike in its ads or the curly letters of Coca-Cola. Furthermore, viewing a brand as a mere category member does nothing to explain the near-fanatical attachment that the successful so-called "cult brands" generate from their buyers nor the tremendous power exerted by the up-and-coming brands like Samsung, Dolce & Gabbana, and Jimmy Choo over our purchase decisions.

Throughout the ages every society has had its peculiar talismans – symbolic objects of public veneration and supposed magical properties that both the mighty and lowly sought to acquire for divine grace, riches, power, luck, and miscellaneous earthly benefits. In fact, assorted charms, amulets, relics, icons, rings, and precious stones have been in continuous use, to work such presumed wonders on their owners from the times of Pharaonic Egypt until the present day. However, as religion and ritual magic have become increasingly separated and de-emphasized from the daily workings of a modern, secular, industrial, and consumerist culture, something else has stepped in to serve the purpose of talismans: a commercial brand.

To say that brands wield such power in our societies would be a flagrant under-statement. Our everyday lives, starting from breakfast and morning news-show and ending with the nightly cup of hot chocolate, revolve around the appreciation, usage, and consumption of numerous brands, each of which has been designed to serve a particular functional purpose but offers a plethora of subtle and supplementary meanings. The business executive who wears a Patek Philippe watch or the Japanese office lady (as she is called in Asia) who flaunts her new Louis Vuitton bag would readily agree that their newly acquired objects bring them joy, prestige, confidence, and maybe even some luck. The same could be said for the teenager sporting an iPod or the terrorist armed with a Kalashnikov. Just like medieval talismans, individuals are willing to toss them aside if they have outlived the purpose or do not deliver the desired benefits. And like talismans, brands also have an inexplicable, dark side. People are willing to go to extreme lengths to possess one if it cannot be acquired legitimately. Teenagers have been known to kill one another for Nike shoes, and young Asian and East European women from respectable, middle-class families have been reported to work as call-girls only to afford a French or Italian designer dress.

To understand how and why brands turn into such societal talismans and why they can extract rabid customer loyalty one day to lose it the next, one has to dig deeper to seek richer and perhaps more philosophical meanings of brands. In Chapter 4, we shall provide our own interpretation of how brands ought to be viewed today, which better explains their functional and dysfunctional appeal, but for now let us consider the widely known interpretations. Most such explanations consider the innate symbolism of the brand's visual identity (name, logo, colors, etc.) and the associations that stem from it and from the perceived quality of its product and service offering. In the end, a brand becomes a handy mnemonic, a cryptogram, or nonsense word (like Kodak and Exxon) that stands for a host of meanings. Every child in America and elsewhere knows that Nike was the Greek goddess of victory and the swoosh signals motion or progress. People around the world look at the golden arch logo of McDonald's and think of cheap, ready-made food, fast and friendly service, and also perhaps the risk of obesity.

Another view of a brand holds that it acts as a living link to history. Coca-Cola and Procter & Gamble in the U.S., Mitsukoshi (department stores) and Kikkoman (soy sauce) in Japan, Harrods and Fortnum & Mason in the U.K., Louis Vuitton and Dom Perignon in France, Siemens and Mercedes-Benz in Germany, and Tiger Balm in Singapore all represent products that are living legends in their countries whose histories have spanned a hundred or more years and each has an anecdotal record passed over generations. Mercedes-Benz with its world-famous three-pointed-star badge indicates reliability and excellence, and evokes in the mind of a connoisseur images of a rich history replete with memories of its many famous and infamous drivers and passengers. Tiger Balm, trusted by generations of Asian families as a miracle cure for all kinds of pains and aches, is said to have originated from a traditional Chinese remedy to cure an emperor's backaches arising of his frequent nocturnal pursuits.

Brand mystique – a fragile asset

For all of its historical and symbolic weight, the mystique of a brand – its indefinable appeal, allure, and cachet amongst the buying public – is a rather delicate and ethereal commodity. It is based on notions such as workmanship, service, trust, respect, and credibility with the customer base, but rather like an individual's personal reputation it is built gradually over time but can be easily and irrevocably lost. Yet, brand mystique is that subtle and essential quality that makes one brand more winning than another; that allows Porsche to draw higher margins over most other cars; that goads people to wait on a chilly night to acquire the latest Playstation; that causes Russian shoppers to stampede to get into an Ikea store; and that inspires a homemaker to pay more for the Surf or Tide detergent instead of a store label. Entire businesses and the livelihoods of many people are built on brand mystique. In fact, while the product offering may change in form and style, and manufacturing techniques may shift over time, brands that retain their mystique, as Nivea, Louis Vuitton, and Krug champagne have done, tend to endure and thrive.

Note that we favor the term "brand mystique" over the two more frequently heard and somewhat equivalent phrases "brand image" and "brand equity". The word "image" seems a bit prosaic and shallow in nearness to the richness of the brand idea. It also does not convey those inexplicable, near-mystical qualities that those "cult brands" like Apple possess, indeed to such an extent that their zealous followers can have their logos painfully tattooed on their bodies, and they throng in rallies where they chant in unison "Steve (Jobs) is God." Mystique is what kept Apple going during those difficult pre-iPod years when IBM clones seemed to dominate the market. The other term in vogue "brand equity" is more an accounting concept, which is perhaps more *au courant* than the old bookkeeping notion of goodwill, but is still less able to capture the public's qualitative and subjective interpretations of a brand.

Brand mystique is all encompassing of the parent firm's activities and has far-reaching consequences. It encapsulates the *totality* of the known information about the brand or firm that resides in the public mind, and that derives from how it looks and works, its past designs, advertisements, endorsers, geographic origins, salient events in its history, and so on. While such meanings should be specific to every individual's personal and idiosyncratic relationship with the brand, they can be generalized at the broader societal level to have a significant impact on its fortunes. Take the case of Snow Brand in Japan. Till early 2002, it was the leading dairy products business in Japan, drawing from its wholesome Hokkaido (northern island, noted for its natural scenery) association and being a perennial favorite of Japanese families. Snow Brand's milk, cheese, and butter products had the highest shares in their respective markets, and the firm had successfully diversified into other categories as well. Then, in January 2002 the company was accused of having falsified its beef labels and having passed off Australian beef as Japanese beef to claim government compensation. This had happened after a major milk poisoning incident. Within a month it was alleged that Snow Brand had even falsified its butter labels to extend them past their expiration dates. In a culture where honesty and integrity are considered inviolable norms, such instances of corporate malfeasance automatically damaged the brand's cachet and credibility and drastically plummeted its sales in all categories. The company went into a rapid tailspin, having to sell off several subsidiaries to its rivals and is only recently making a slow comeback.

Considering therefore that brand mystique is such a valuable asset, one would think that companies would go to extreme lengths to build it, retain it, and certainly not dilute or weaken it. While the Snow Brand situation represents an extreme case, examples abound where firms have allowed their brands to be diluted through their own marketing actions and saw the repercussions on their overall businesses. Ford attempted to increase sales of its newly acquired Jaguar division by extending it to the middle-market to impress a younger buyer. The resulting model, the $30,000 X-Type sedan, so resembled the down-market Ford Mondeo in its stodgy and compressed shape that it offended the core enthusiasts for whom Jaguar is a byword for sleekness and style. The car did not catch on even among the novice buyers. Some say that the X-Type has forever ruined the mystique of owning a Jaguar. Similar criticisms are also heard among European car puritans about Porsche and its Cayenne sport-utility-vehicle. They feel that Porsche has over-catered to the wealthy, suburban American buyer with this seeming monstrosity, which is an affront to the sporting heritage of Porsche.

For firms that sell luxury, it is an absolute imperative to preserve the brand mystique, which is the sum total of their businesses. Else, why would someone spend princely sums, more than the average annual incomes of people in most countries, to buy their watches, stay in their hotels, take their first-class flights, cruises, and so on? By far, the biggest threat to brand mystique for an up-market luxury or fashion item is over-exposure. The clientèle would be turned off if the brand was seen as being too visible, too eager to make profits, too readily accessible or associated with the "wrong" type of customer. The famed Krug champagne, now owned by LVMH, has retained its mystique over time because it has discreetly shunned over-publicity, choosing to limit the production, and pricing itself in the bracket of exclusive fine wines. Krug is operated by the sixth generation of the eponymous family and reportedly tastes the same as it did in 1843, when the company was founded. In contrast, Pierre Cardin, once a respected French apparel label, no longer retains its allure and cachet. The label's overuse of licensing of a large number of seemingly unrelated products and accessories of questionable quality has cheapened the brand itself. Meanwhile, Mercedes, Rolex, Burberry, and Louis Vuitton have had problems of their own in maintaining their prestige status as they have perhaps become too popular for their own good. In America the computer-seller Gateway, which now finds itself in dire straits, changed its sales strategy so many times that consumers were not just confused – they lost track what the brand meant and eventually they did not care. A wag once quipped that Gateway has dallied with more models than the billionaire proprietor Donald Trump.

Brand dilution is a very subtle and long-drawn process that is inscrutable till it is too late. The end is usually a precipitous decline when a firm notices customers defecting in droves and faces opprobrium in the media and from consumer groups. A downfall like this can be so swift and severe in instances that it seems to defy a fundamental business truism, that the weight of the brand itself should present a bulwark against adversity. But, nearly always, brand failure had preceded, and indeed presaged business failure, and the brand failed because it had become devalued and corroded over time. This chapter lays out a principal cause why this happens – over-marketing, and its attendant vice, over-catering to customers.

The perils of over-marketing

The great Taoist philosopher Lao Tzu once said that a large country must be governed like one cooks small fish – delicately. The more one stirs and churns, the messier is usually the result. There is a somewhat parallel culinary metaphor in the Western world that too many cooks end up spoiling the broth. Such dictums should be applied to how to manage a great brand – because so many of them have been diluted and damaged by their own managers – not from apathy or want of attention but indeed from *too much* intervention. Over-exposure in the media, over-aggressive push marketing, over-extensions, over-franchising, too many ads and sales promotions, too many strategic "corrections" and tactical implementations, all of these have diminished the qualities that stood in lieu of the brand in the first place.

Marks & Spencer, Disney, Sears, Levi's, Ford, Pierre Cardin, Swissair, Tommy Hilfiger, and Gap were once magical names that commanded both respect and admiration, such that they were near-automatic consumer choices in their categories. But today many of these brands languish and ail in a sea of profit warnings and negative public perceptions – and some appear to have been irrevocably damaged. Coca-Cola was once hailed as an exemplar of savvy marketing and global branding finesse. It now has a serious image problem in Europe and the Americas. In Britain, the press and consumer groups criticized the company for attempting to portray its Dasani bottled water brand as mineral water when in reality it is purified tap water. Coke executives have not ceased to push their cola beverages when the present trends of increasing health consciousness dictate they shift emphasis to water and fruit drinks instead. In Disney's case, its iconic animation characters are not the same draw among children as in the past. Mickey Mouse and Donald Duck do not excite kids' imaginations the way they used to before. For this, the firm has to blame itself for its unfettered commercialism and gross over-merchandising, all of which have effectively washed off the magical appeal of these characters.

Not so long ago, Tommy Hilfiger was viewed as a trendy and fashionable brand symbolizing urban American chic. Then, the familiar storyline played itself out. Success was followed by over-expansion, resulting in too many "flagship" stores and miscellaneous accessories, thereby causing brand depletion, and finally losses and store closures. Similarly, Boston Chicken (later renamed Boston Market) exemplifies the perils of over-marketing very aptly. At one time, this restaurant-style fast food chain was very successful – in fact, the fastest growing franchise in America. But by growing so fast the company took on massive debt, which it could not repay. The firm became bankrupt and sold out (to McDonald's) just as quickly it had started. The Dockers brand of trouser became the nemesis of the iconic Levi's label, as its attempt to dress the boomers in loose-fitting pants turned off the younger generation, who did not want to be seen in their dad's choice of clothes.

During the 2005 American Super-Bowl, the Ford Motor Company spent a prodigious amount of money placing commercials throughout the entire game. However, in several instances the *same* Ford ad-clips appeared consecutively that seemed to many viewers as being silly and desperate, particularly at a time when the company's plight was widely known to the public.

Not so long ago, Nike's overuse of star (Michael Jordan, Charles Barkley, Spike Lee, etc.) endorsements and its loud, in-your-face advertising had the counter-productive effect of attracting widespread public and press attention to itself and its business practices. Subsequent news reports of sweatshop labor among some of its subcontractors angered the young, socially conscious buyers, and led to a serious image problem that the company has had to painstakingly correct. Lately, Nike has visibly toned down its marketing and advertising in the popular media. Instead, it attempts to influence the youth through more subtle messages like endorsements of sports events and displaying its logo on popular athletes but without overstating the association.

The major consumer goods and cereal makers, like Procter & Gamble and General Mills, have sharply cut back their price incentives in weekend newspaper inserts because they have found that giving such coupons and "dollar off" deals tend to make the buyer deal-prone, and therefore less loyal. Buyers tend to internalize the lower price they pay when they have such a deal as being the "fair price" for these well-known national brands. Consequently, when the price promotions are not offered, they think that the companies are exacting *more* than their due margins, and flock *en masse* to purchasing store brands instead. It is true to say that over-couponing and excessive price promotions have disrupted the habitual buying pattern of many shoppers in a way that is detrimental to major brands.

Mercedes-Benz has a premium, luxury image in the U.S., unlike in its native Germany. One, however, wonders how long this image will hold, considering its executives are seemingly shooting themselves in the foot having introduced a series of down-market models, like the A, B, C, and E classes to attract a younger, less-affluent buyer. A rather inept Mercedes commercial that used to be aired on American TV networks showed a woman delivering newspapers in an upscale neighborhood from her C-Class! While the E-Class has been a worldwide success, in our view DaimlerChrysler should have stopped there and not ventured downward, since one can only surmise the harm the lower models have caused to the flagship's mystique and prestige status. Indeed, traditional owners of the S-Class, represented usually by the so-called "old money" and the corporate set, are often bemused, if somewhat peeved, to see college students driving an automobile with the same three-pointed star. Not surprisingly, those who have money to spend and who wish to own a truly exclusive make are now opting to own a Bentley or an Aston Martin instead.

We believe that the mistake that these companies have made has been in over-doing their traditional marketing tactics. Marketing, which had unfailingly delivered revenues before, became seen as the ultimate short-term panacea for all business problems. Accordingly, the firms joined in for a wholesale overkill: new stores, new products, brand extensions, category extensions, heavy promotion (both ad and coupons) campaigns, reckless use of brand ambassadors, and so on. If one were to chart the progression of brands over the last century, one would find an upwardly trending curve lasting till the late 1980s and early 1990s. Then something different and drastic happened. Many well-known, one-iconic brands underwent a serious reversal of fortunes that cannot be explained by sheer market, economy, or technology dynamics. We have seen more catastrophic business failures in recent years than at any time in history, except perhaps during the Great Depression. But, other firms have performed very well in the same period. If one were to look at history, one would find that the corporations that went from small to great grew very patiently and deliberately over many years. Their founders and executives acted like devoted stewards, showing parent-like care, painstakingly weighing every business decision and growth opportunity with caution and prudence. Regrettably, that caution has been thrown into the wind since the mid-1980s because over-marketing is usually the outcome of managerial impatience and a lack of prudence.

The downside of over-catering to customers

The new reverse psychology marketing game says, "Don't run after customers. Let them come to you instead." This may sound positively heretical to an average marketing person. But, in truth, a number of firms are doing just that today, having chosen to renounce their past practices of giving promotions and freebies to corral incidental buyers, who in the end turned out to be fickle and exited at the prospect of a better deal. There is a growing and pervasive sense among senior executives that following the ephemeral whims and fanciful demands of such unreliable customers have led many companies into a morass of high costs, lost managerial focus, and depleted brand image. The American car companies have lost their pricing power and their brand cachets by handing out billions of dollars in rebates and buyer incentives over the years, which have only reinforced the market's perception that they cannot sell otherwise. Since the mid-1980s, firms have strayed from their core missions and lost their internal discipline as "marketing by focus groups" began to take hold within their business cultures. Many organizations utilized such customer input to decide how they should tailor their offering, what kind of new product they should launch, what should be the ad message, and so on. While this practice may sound sensible in theory, in practice the results have been counterproductive at best and disastrous at worst.

Critics and movie audiences complain that Hollywood movie studios have become risk-averse and less creative in recent times, and more prone to enacting sequels and safe and predictable themes, like animated cartoons and action extravaganzas. It is widely known that movies are heavily customized, their endings and storylines adapted, depending on the opinions of a test audience of selected viewers. Marketing has also been accused of compromising the artistic and substantive merit of books and magazines, as authors and publishers have focused more on over-catering to their readership to increase selling potential. Some have seen in this a decline in the quality and impact of literature, poetry, and general writing. The apparel chain Gap found that pursuing the fickle trends of what it assumed was the latest in fashion and style damaged the reputation it had among its core buyers for casual and basic clothing – the company is still recovering from its past missteps. Tommy Hilfiger, Planet Hollywood, and the Gap once had cult-like appeal among the youth. Each suffered a loss in image as they attempted to over-sell to the buyer, by seeking to over-customize its offerings and by over-distributing through more channels and more locations.

Consider in this context the rise and the subsequent decline of CNN in the U.S. In its early days Cable News Network or CNN, as it is known to the whole world, was considered the purveyor of "hard news" and truly global coverage, both rarities in American network television. It was a channel unlike any other – 24-hour news from around the world improvised by a small group of quirky but dedicated anchors, who paid less attention to style but more to the news content that they were broadcasting. CNN rapidly gained a cult-like following among educated urbanites. Its niche but loyal audience enjoyed the in-depth coverage of the world that the major networks did not carry, going by the (flawed) conventional wisdom that it is uninteresting to the American public.

Over time, however, CNN became more mainstream and marketing-oriented, and started to tailor its news and programs to what they thought the broader American audience wanted. Perhaps, its managers relied too heavily on focus groups and market surveys, or perhaps, they wanted to emulate the major networks and become a mainstream player. All the same, very soon, it began to resemble the other networks, with newly recruited attractive-looking anchors and their usual, familiar, chatty on-air approach. While it may have enjoyed a period of success from a larger audience and consequently higher ad revenues, CNN quickly lost the support of its *core* viewer-base. Indeed, it effectively left a wide opening for another competitor to come in, in this instance Rupert Murdoch's Fox News, to occupy its previously vacated slot for hard news coverage. Now, the net result is that CNN has a declining viewership while Fox News goes from strength to strength.

No one in his right mind will ever say that caring for the customer is unimportant for a business. But the mistake that many firms made was to put too much stock in the credo "getting bigger is better" and that *all* customers are created equal. As the CNN and Gap examples illustrate, the firm is better off catering to its core customer above all others, and in remaining true to its intrinsic product philosophy. The other mistake was that businesses decided that the customer should dictate critical product development, service design, and ad content decisions. The problem with this view is that the customer often does not know and cannot predict what he or she will like. Jerry Seinfeld, the protagonist of the eponymous TV comedy that attained a phenomenal level of worldwide success, reportedly hangs the page from the audience feedback of his pilot in his bathroom. The subjects had apparently castigated the whole concept.

It is an accepted and well-understood fact among marketing researchers that people are notorious predictors of their own behavior – what they say in questionnaires is not borne out by what they actually *do*. Firms therefore have had to suffer the cruel irony of having earned high scores on customer satisfaction surveys and still experience large-scale customer defections to a lower-priced competitor. Besides, most people are good at thinking only incrementally, that is in conceptualizing small improvements to existing things and product ideas, and then in opining how these changes may fare in practice. They are far less adept at fathoming the impact and potential of the truly major leaps in technology and knowledge, those that have the capacity to revolutionalize society and transform lives. That leads us to an intrinsic but far more insidious fallacy of consumer focus groups. An over-reliance on their feedback and supposed wisdom can lead firms to opt for safer paths, such as a predictable brand extension (e.g., soap to shampoo, jewelry to watch, etc.) or a product sequel of the "new and improved" kind. Critics claim that compared to today the start of the last century saw more breakthrough inventions and path-breaking business ideas. After all, Edison, Graham Bell, and Sears did not use focus groups.

Why do firms over-market?

From the above discussion, it has become quite clear that over-marketing is usually counter-productive and detrimental to brand value and general business health. So then, why do it? The short answer is it is so easy. Opening one more store or granting yet another license to a partner is a small and marginal investment, whose results are immediately visible on the bottom line. It is also very tempting. When an entrepreneur or business has a new product success, the pressure to grow it quickly is huge. Vera Bradley, an Indiana-based business founded by two women, is a highly successful maker of colorful and feminine bags and purses. Now, the firm plans to venture into dolls, sunglasses, baby accessories, and men's items – with questionable wisdom and predictable consequences.

For entrepreneurs and corporations alike, there is always a nagging pressure from investors, board members, and Wall Street analysts to show a pattern of ever-higher earnings and revenue growth. Managers are also an impatient and ambitious bunch, eager to demonstrate their marketing acumen and business savvy. Many, especially those that are fresh from an MBA program, nurse somewhat dreamy ideas about the efficacy of marketing. In truth, marketing is not a panacea, but needs to be managed and controlled in a thoughtful way for maximum brand and business benefit. To steward a business to growth and maturity over time takes considerable patience and dedication. Splurging investor dollars on high-profile TV ads and rapid-fire gimmicks to make a splash, push, and sell may result in increased publicity and short-term sales but usually has dubious longer-term consequences. The ploys that are usually on display on Donald Trump's (and Sir Alan Sugar's) *The Apprentice* television show tend only to reinforce the stereotypes about impatient young managers engaging in short-term thinking and their hard-driving bosses egging them on.

Perhaps, the fault lies less with managers but more with the over-aching paradigm itself. This paradigm enjoins a business to engage in a relentless pursuit of revenues and profits, the idea being that it eventually benefits the shareholders, which is the *summum bonum* – the greatest good – of a free-market system. Thus, we have had more and more GM cars and car models, more Boston Market stores, and more accessories bearing the Pierre Cardin label, and so on. In the beginning, each additional product, store, and category extension is viewed positively by customers, perhaps as a benefit or a convenience, and the results are therefore reflected in the firm's bottom line. Hence, the conventional thinking that "more is better" seems validated and marketing is viewed as having achieved its purpose and then managers and shareholders have reasons to be content. Over time, however, disturbing indicators begin to appear. As more products are launched, more stores opened, and more licenses awarded, overall revenues may still look to be growing but the marginal increase from each additional activity shows a clear declining trend. Toward the end, overall sales level out and actually start to fall and very soon the entire business is in dire peril.

Figure 2.1 illustrates the life cycle of a modern-day business. The curve showing brand mystique, as gauged by the market, acts as a leading indicator and

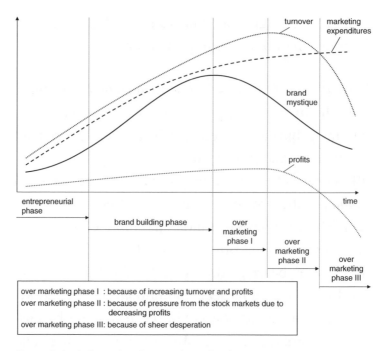

Figure 2.1   Life cycle of a modern-day business

anticipates the sales and profitability trends. To a manager, expenditures on marketing seem to correlate highly and positively to turnover till the critical inflection point is reached, when everything seems to go awry. More and more dollars spent on marketing schemes no longer deliver the promised returns. Instead, the correlation with sales and profits changes to negative. Firms may then implement a variety of over-marketing tactics in sheer desperation, such as relaunching the brand and buying expensive airtime on television – usually, to little avail.

The above pattern is so commonplace and pervasive, yet it is a mystery why it is allowed to be repeated. Perhaps, the motto of "get big fast" is inscribed, like some preordained business commandment, in the brain of every budding entrepreneur, every marketing manager, every CEO, and, in short, every businessperson who has experienced the first flush of success. Or, perhaps, the urge to cash in when one has hit on a winning recipe is just too tempting to refuse. Yet, we have seen more rapid creations and failures of businesses since the mid-1970s than at any time in the past. The common theme across many of them was the firm's insatiable thirst for profits, and the failure to assess the sustainable size of the network, that is in not knowing where to draw the line so that brand mystique, always a fragile and fleeting commodity, was not impaired.

The rules of pull marketing

The pull marketing game does not push or foist the product on a hapless customer. Instead, it holds that customers must somehow be allowed to "discover" the product and come to it from their own volition. Making the product functionally clever, its design and service appealing, and its price reasonable, *but without seeming to aggressively sell*, shows off the brand in a special light and attracts the buyer on its own. This can be achieved without the expenditure of costly advertising and promotions. In today's interconnected and consumerist culture, getting publicity and spreading buzz are not typically the problem. There is always enough pent-up demand for an efficient and timely product, and present-day society is adequately "wired" to take word-of-mouth about such a product to an entirely new and vertiginous level. Otherwise, what accounts for the phenomenal success of the Apple iPod, the Motorola Razr phone, the Dyson vacuum cleaner, and *The Da Vinci Code*? And prospective buyers who gravitate to the store, having previously done their investigations on the Internet or been referred to by friends, are already pre-sold.

The ad message, if the firm opts for some advertising, does not have to be of the familiar loud, blatant, and chest-thumping kind. That is calculated to turn off every smart and savvy consumer of today. The German government recently learned an expensive lesson about the universality of this concept when its $30 million "Du bist Deutschland" (you are Germany) ad-blitz ended up as something resembling a fiasco with average Germans. It had started out as a marketing campaign attempting to "sell Germany to the Germans" and showing icons like Beethoven, Einstein, Franz Beckenbauer, and Michael Schumacher encouraging Germans to take more pride in their homeland. Soon, newspaper columnists, net bloggers, and average citizens were complaining about the syrupy sentimentalism and humdrum banality of the ads. The campaign was also not helped by the subsequent discovery that the same slogan was formerly used in Nazi party rallies.

What works in advertising now is the honest, quirky, understated, and minimalist message. The Japanese call it *Zen* advertising, one that focuses on the soft sell and that piques the buyer's interest by making a very subtle, nuanced, and self-effacing statement about the firm and the product. The Land of the Rising Sun has been the origin of many popular, recent business ideas and product fads. Such buzz concepts as the Toyota Production System (TPS), quality circles, *kaizen*, *anime*, *manga*, and *sudoku* had their origins in Japan and now have a world-wide following. Zen advertising is still in its early stages in Europe and the U.S., but one is beginning to see its successful uses. In America the Progressive car insurance company has been running a very effective ad campaign where it openly says it may not offer the best quotes in all cases. It invites buyers to check its website, which has a running ticker showing the actual rates real people are getting on the major insurance carriers. Progressive is not the cheapest in many of these cases. But the element of trust and credibility that this tactic engenders acts as an attractive force in its own right.

The poster children of pull marketing

Finally, let us look at two firms, one from the U.S. and the other from Europe. They are, in our view, the best exemplars of the kind of pull marketing that we have discussed as being the way of the future. Each attracts people by its own merits and does not pressure or aggressively sell. The first example is the search engine Google. Its popularity rests squarely on its understated layout. No pop-up ads, no pressure to buy, no clutter, no fancy graphics – merely a simple format that provides information in a straightforward textual form to user's questions. Google began its life as an effective programmatic tool to make better searches on the web. Its founders Larry Page and Sergey Brin met while they were computer science students at Stanford. They kept the format as simple as possible. They did not base their site on any focus groups. Google does not do any *overt* marketing, such as asking users to officially register and enter any personal information. Everything Google does to make money is behind the scenes, through selling key words to advertisers for contextual ad placement. That beauty of simplicity is in marked contrast with most other portals. Opening the AOL page causes numerous secondary screens to pop up, each urging the user to try different things and peddle new AOL products. Yahoo's screen, on the other hand, is an over-cluttered and bewildering forest of links, which could flummox a novice computer user.

The sole *caveat* we offer about Google is concerning its present, post-IPO life-stage. The soaring stock and all of the financial speculation surrounding it seem to have created a dynamic of its own. Lately, the firm has been in the limelight a little too much, its press releases have become a little too frequent, as it reportedly seeks to engage in a number of ambitious, profit-generating ventures. From the discussion in this chapter, Google ought to be wary about the pit-falls of over-marketing. We are therefore not certain if Google will remain true to its brand mantra "Don't be evil" and if the brand will retain its mystique into the near future.

Some say the Starbucks has pulling power over its loyal clientèle, who could not do without their daily fixes. But the coffee shop that frankly outdoes Starbucks in the novelty of its pull marketing and the affection with which it is held by its customers is Tchibo. Founded in 1949, it is the largest coffee chain in Germany and presently operates in mostly German-speaking countries of Europe. The novelty of a Tchibo shop lies in its unique retail format. Besides selling coffee, each of its shops acts as a fascinating showcase where smart, new products, which are exclusively made for Tchibo by brand name manufacturers, are displayed and sold every week. As the shopper sips her cappuccino, she can browse a limited assortment of clothes, jewelry, kitchen equipment, gadgets, and mobile phones all inside the coffee shop. Tchibo changes the collection every week using the slogan "Every week a new experience". Customers know that if they would like to buy something they would have to act fast since the item quantity is limited and the display changes rapidly. Most purchases are therefore made on impulse. It is a common sight on European sidewalks to see families and tourists peeping at the windows of a Tchibo shop to see what new products have arrived that week. Tchibo has such a devoted following that recently when it introduced prepaid mobile phone service, it quickly emerged as a major player in Germany with more than half a million subscribers in a very short time. Perhaps, the main attraction has to do with the fact that Tchibo's prices are simple and transparent, and the whole selling format is low-pressure and relaxed. After all, coffee is a good relaxing agent.

3

"Wal-Marts and Ferraris"

For a number of decades, it was quite normal to find in most product categories *three* clearly discernible tiers of products and services. Each category had a series of items positioned at various price points within the discount segment; there was a huge selection in the middle-market segment, and a large, but not excessive, number of brands in the luxury segment. From the consumer's point of view, there was more than an adequate quantity of products and offerings available – with new ones joining them every month or year. Within each tier, only a few products, however, really had their own autonomous profile, a distinct brand identity, so the consumers predictably lost track of things and were merely confused by all these developments. A prospective buyer saw no further point in paying more for certain higher-priced items when there were no longer any salient differences compared with less expensive ones belonging to the same tier. This three-way split, however, seems now to have disappeared. The conventional three-tier structure has mutated in many product categories into two highly *polarizing* market niches – "hard-discount" and "premium luxury".

The middle-market segment looks like it has suddenly ceased to exist – one may say, caved in – because the products and brands in this segment simply showed too little identity or profile. This phenomenon is ongoing and can be observed in both the consumer goods and the industrial sectors.

There is a specter hanging over the consumer and industrial markets in nearly all developed economies. Many companies that were positioned to compete in the erstwhile middle market have either become defunct or are finding their survival gravely threatened in the changing business dynamic. As a result, they have resorted to copying the tactics of firms in the discount segment. Yet, at one time not too long ago, the prospects of these middle-tier firms looked so stable and secure, as they seemed to offer the best value to their buyers, this being the most acceptable compromise between price and quality. Sears, the bastion of middle-market retailers in the U.S., was the classic all-American brand – the average American family's weekend destination for clothes, appliances, and hardware. How the fortunes change! Sears' future now looks bleak and young people of today would be hard-pressed to identify Bob Vila, who was once its iconic TV handyman, and who still appears in some of its commercials. Likewise, in Britain, teenage girls once dreamed of securing a job as a salesgirl at a Marks & Spencer. It is now said that the first few words that babies there learn to utter nowadays are Mum, Dad, and Tesco.

From a success perspective, it seems that lately there are only two competing stories emerging from the financial presses day after day. On the one hand, gargantuan profits from the discounters – the Wal-Marts, Tescos, Lidls, and Ikeas of the world – and on the other hand, similarly hefty earnings in the premium luxury segment – the LVMHs, Richemonts, Porsches, and Ferraris in various sectors. Besides profitability, these companies at the discount and the luxury ends are also successful in other key areas, for example risk-taking, product innovation, revenue growth, and as employment hubs. In stark contrast, middle-market firms that were once healthy, profitable, growing, and attractive to young people – the Mujis, Marks & Spencers, Sears, Alitalias, and Schwabs of the world – are increasingly facing painful and traumatic restructuring as they make the transition to a new and untested business model in order to compete and survive.

Many consumer and several industrial markets can now be characterized as being composed of "Wal-Marts and Ferraris". On the one hand, we have the discounters (in various degrees of "hardness") such as Lidl, Dollar General, Southwest Airlines, TD Ameritrade brokerage, and Ikea, which focus on satisfying the mainly *functional quality* needs of their buyers, albeit at highly competitive prices. Their shoppers are prepared to accept many inconveniences, such as little or no service, low product availability and long waits, in order to avail of their discount prices. At the other end, we have the premium luxury brands, such as Gucci, Bulgari, Porsche, and assorted charter airlines, which are very expensive but offer the absolute and uncompromising best in quality. This is usually done in the form of the ultimate in design and service – that is *soft quality*. Their buyers also secure the satisfaction and the prestige of owning a status symbol. Obviously, to do it effectively the luxury product must meet these criteria to a T. The two segments – discount and luxury – are the principal beneficiaries of the unfolding business scenario.

What is the best way of characterizing this trend, described here in general terms, toward the two extreme positions across multiple product and service categories? For the sake of illustration, we provide several concrete examples of this far-reaching development below.

1. Wal-Mart, the world's largest retailer, reports billions of dollars of profits each year and is growing at such a frenetic pace all over the world that unnerves not just its fledgling competitors, but also national lawmakers, local government officials, and community activists. For better or for worse, the company has driven countless mom-and-pop stores out of business in the U.S. and elsewhere, as well as quite a few category-killers (Toys "R" Us being a prime example). Its procurement process is an absolute beauty, designed to eliminate the modicum of wastage and to

secure maximum advantage for its own end in a way that would do credit to even the most efficient armies in history. Wal-Mart's biggest asset is its monstrous size, whereby its ever-increasing volume of purchases extracts submissive concessions from suppliers in a self-reinforcing, virtuous pattern. In an interesting parallel (testifying no doubt to the universality of the model's success potential), Tesco of the U.K., Carrefour of France, Aldi, Lidl, and Schlecker of Germany, as well as Daiso's 100-yen stores and the *combinis* of Japan (such as Seven-Eleven) have followed a near-identical *leitmotif*. As a result, once venerable shopping icons for the middle-class, such as Sears (of the U.S.), Marks & Spencer, Boots, and Dixon's (of the U.K.), Karstadt (of Germany), and Daiei (of Japan), find their positions gravely imperilled.

2. Meanwhile, the absolute high-end department stores (Neiman-Marcus, Bloomingdale's, Saks, Nordstrom, KaDeWe, and Galeries Lafayette) and luxury fashion houses have seen no adverse impact on their revenues whatsoever. Indeed, sales of luxury products such as apparel, jewelry, watches, leather goods, and wines are at an all-time high. The British label Burberry experienced a remarkable turnaround in its fortunes under its last CEO. The firm is now actually attempting to *curb* the cult-like popularity of its trademarked camel-plaid scarves, caps, and bags among certain consumers in Britain lest they taint the reputation of the brand (more on this in Chapter 4).

Bulgari, the century-plus old jeweler to the aristocracy, has seen its sales jump ten-fold between the early 1990s and the start of the 21st century. Its prospects have never looked better, as the increasingly affluent Chinese, Indian and Russian women look fondly toward the famed European marques and away from the locally-available alternatives.

3. The airline industry faces the same dynamic as discounters like Southwest in the U.S., Ryanair and easyJet in Europe, Gol in Brazil, Virgin Blue in Australia, and Air Deccan in India continue to chomp at the market shares of the established, middle-market carriers. These discount airlines presume only to satisfy the core or functional needs of their passengers. Their customers are willing to accept plenty of inconvenience (e.g., booking via internet only, no seat assignments, no meals, etc.) merely to avail of a highly competitive price. Hence, middle-tier carriers, such as Japan Airlines, Swiss, Austrian, Iberia, Air India, SAS, Qantas, and Alitalia, all face growing challenges over many of their most profitable routes. The competitive pressure is proving disastrous for legacy U.S. carriers like American, Delta, United, and USAir that have also had jet fuel and low capacity problems to deal with since 2001. Nonetheless, the fact remains that Southwest and Ryanair have contended with similar pervasive worldwide problems, but are thriving chiefly because of their Wal-Mart-like efficiencies. At the opposite end of the airline sector,

recent years have seen a burgeoning growth of its own "Ferraris", namely the super-exclusive, top-dollar charter jets that cater mostly to companies and very affluent individuals. These boutique air-carriers offer the ultimate level of service, including private airport connections, Michelin star-rated meals, and hotel-like amenities on board.

4. Similar to mass-merchandise retailing, the food-retailing business in America and Europe has fragmented quite clearly between those shoppers who prefer the everyday low prices at a Wal-Mart, Aldi, Lidl, or Food Basics versus others who are increasingly looking to pay top prices for organic, non-genetically modified (GM) food-stuffs. At the discount supermarkets, customers have to put up with many inconveniences, such as an untidy presentation, limited selection, absence of well-known brands, difficulty of finding store-clerks to seek assistance, and so on. Yet, this sector manages to thrive just the same. Consequently, those remaining middle-market firms are now trying to imitate the strategy of the discounters – they too advertise low prices and offer regular price cuts. What they cannot do, however, is achieve the same consistent image (as that of the hard discounters) in the eyes of consumers. Their sales strategy seems to develop in fits and starts, extolling the virtues of their superior service on one day and of their low prices on another. To a shopper, it all appears incoherent and a bit confusing. From a financial

standpoint, it is universally understood that the middle-market firms cannot achieve the same level of success – in profit terms – because they have an entirely different and much less efficient cost structure as compared to the hard discounters. It is therefore a logical development that many middle-tier firms in the food sector should face serious problems in the U.S. and Europe. At the other end of the scale – the premium food sector – things are entirely different. The meteoric rise of the Austin-based Whole Foods Market in the U.S., which mainly sells organic, non-GM produce, testifies to a burgeoning marketing phenomenon. Whole Foods, dubbed in the media as "Whole Paycheck" for its propensity to charge top-dollar prices for all its items, still manages to thrive when many far less expensive food-markets are going out of business. As a general trend, of course, all sorts of natural and non-industrial products are gaining increasing worldwide favor. This development is discussed in more detail in Chapter 5.

5. The beauty-care industry has not avoided the phenomenon of the embattled middle-market. These days, when American and European women shop for cosmetics, they increasingly look to buy the inexpensive drugstore versions for their daily use. In Europe, the very successful drugstore chain "dm" offers its own private label, called Balea, as a cheaper substitute for the well-known Nivea brand. Balea products (and their packaging) resemble Nivea

very closely, and are enjoying comparable success as a cheap, everyday alternative. For special occasions, however, women are not content with the erstwhile "safe", middle-tier likes of Revlon and Estée Lauder. Instead, even middle-class shoppers have been shelling out tidy sums to buy the *really* expensive, high-end brands like Procter & Gamble's SK-II that costs up to $300 and is sold only at exclusive department stores.

6. The apparel category shows a very similar development. Teenagers in Europe and the U.S. who are looking to buy jeans usually settle for an inexpensive private-label version (like H&M, Mango, Zara, or J.C. Penney's a.n.a) or, if the situation demands, a boutique or designer brand (like Diesel or Dolce & Gabbana) that is intended to impress peers. As in all of the above cases, only the brands at the far ends of the apparel market are experiencing true economic success. Consequently, those that still remain in the middle market face a perilous position. The question then is whether these brands can conceivably move up from the middle-tier to the luxury end, or will they inevitably slide downward to the discount sector. As we have emphasized in Chapter 2, achieving the former is quite difficult and, in fact, almost impossible if it is the same label. Middle-tier brands, like Gap and Levi's, cannot shake off the image that they have accrued over many years and be able to join the exalted ranks of premium brands with no apparent hitch. Toyota

was able to do that in the car industry (see below) only by offering an entirely different brand and quality level, Lexus. And, even so, Toyota went to extraordinary lengths to keep the connection hidden for a time. But the weight of historical evidence suggests that most consumer brands fail to complete that crucial leap from the middle-tier to premium luxury. Given this scenario, the position becomes precarious for something as middle-of-the-road as Levi's is in the jeans category. After a series of over-marketing missteps, Levi's has lately resorted to joining the ranks of discounters in the U.S. Its brand is now sold at Wal-Mart.

7. The above pattern has repeated itself for people buying cars. Many car buyers in the U.S. and Europe have been attracted by the bargain prices that are available on the low-end versions of the perennial favorites – Toyota, Honda, and Nissan – and on the new models from the up-and-coming discount brands, such as Hyundai, Kia, Skoda, and Dacia. Perhaps, ultra-cheap Chinese models like Geely and Chery will win the day in the not-too-distant future. This end of the spectrum is clearly getting crowded. And it will not be easy for those firms that have remained in the middle to enter this market. The losers in this picture are likely to be the American carmakers, who continue to suffer from an undeserved stigma of low quality and a somewhat less undeserved perception of bad designs. In marked contrast, at the luxury end, the top-end

marques – typically, the Porsches, Ferraris, Aston Martins, and Bentleys are being selected in large numbers by the younger, newly prosperous buyers. Often, in this revised equation, not all of Toyota's Lexus and Nissan's Infiniti brands do not count for true luxury, for which the firms have only themselves to blame for having confused the buyers with a succession of cheaper models.

8. Finally, many of the mature industrial markets have not escaped the traumas of the disappearing middle market causing firms in the steel, print, leather goods, textiles, and chemicals industries to either go out of business or to have to find new ways of competing. For example, in the steel industry, firms are now clearly split down the middle between those that produce cheaper, low-grade steel and those European and Japanese makers that earn much higher margins by selling the customized, high-end type. Theoretically, companies in industrial categories with endangered middle-markets face two possibilities. The first (apart from the obvious option to close down) is to try to beat the discount segment by joining them, that is move production to countries with lower cost regions (e.g., Asia or Eastern Europe) and attempt to stay competitive. The risk lies here from the diffusion of critical expertise and know-how to those countries and it will only be a matter of time before Asian or Eastern European manufacturers approach the Western markets with their own competitive offerings.

The second possibility is to aim for the high-end. Of course, production in the high-end segment has also moved to countries with low wage costs. But there is still a long time before their local brands can effectively compete on the world stage at the top end. And it is relatively easier for middle-tier *industrial* firms to make the transition to the upper echelons of their markets since they are less tied down by their brand status than the consumer goods firms. One instance of a successful crossover to the high-end segment is the case of Italian textile firms. Their story exemplifies how many previously middle-tier industrial firms are coping with the changing market dynamic. These family-owned Italian companies that traditionally sold to clients in the U.S. and Europe have found that the relentless, price-based competition from low-wage countries in Asia take away a significant part of their business. To survive, these firms have successfully retooled themselves to sell *only* in the high-margin, specialized textiles and garments niches.

What are the reasons for these trends? Why is the middle hollowing out in many product categories?

There is a whole set of reasons for the trend away from the old three-segment market structure – discount, middle-market, and premium – and toward two very much polarizing – hard discount and premium luxury segments. Some of these reasons relate to the growing significance of discount and luxury products themselves, while the others have more to do with why there is no room left in the center, that is in the past middle-market.

1. *China*: If there is one word that is the number one reason for the present state of the markets, this is the one. The end of the last century oversaw the steady rise of China to become a global manufacturing hub for all sorts of consumer and industrial products ranging from high-end technology (DVD players, laptops, color TVs) and "white good" appliances (refrigerators, washing-machines, etc.) to cheaper goods like toys, kitchen utensils, and batteries. In fact, Chinese suppliers account for the vast majority of everyday products sold in the developed and developing world under familiar Western brand names. Consequently, for most people, the "made in China" label is no longer an object of derision or aversion. The cheaper yet functionally good Chinese-made products are winning over buyers everywhere much to the chagrin of the traditional quality- and service-oriented middle-tier firms. Indeed, one may say that the true secret to the spectacular success of Wal-Mart and other super retailers is the humble Chinese daily-wage worker who produces most of its offerings. China's reach extends to all corners of the market. Even categories that were previously considered high-end or luxury have not

been exempt from the profit-hungry eyes of the Chinese entrepreneur. For instance, the Matsu-take mushrooms (traditional Japanese delicacy) that are sold in Tokyo are now largely impor-ted from China because the Chinese have man-aged to undercut the local producers. It is also an open secret that many upmarket brand-makers of apparel, athletic shoes, and leather accessories have production facilities in China, and in the neighboring low-wage countries. The next sub-stantial development, and one which is already imminent, is that Chinese companies will start pushing their way into Western markets with their own homegrown brands. The first examples of this have already been provided by the Haier products, Lenovo notebooks, and the Bao Steel group. Similar developments are also already forthcoming in the automobile market – the first Chinese car models for the European market were presented last year at the Frankfurt Motor Show.

2. *The "good enough" effect*: Consumers today, especially the younger ones, are savvier and more willing to take a risk since they think that the large multinational firms usually charge a "brand premium" to pay for their higher advert-ising budgets. "Why should I pay for the label if everything is made in China?" is therefore a common refrain. Many consider the low-priced Wal-Mart version to be good enough for their everyday needs. In truth, they are not far off the mark because the rapid spread of technology in many industries has resulted in widespread

product commodification, which in turn implies that the Wal-Mart version is not bad, at least not in functional quality terms. Young American college-goers have become acquainted with Haier appliances, usually bought from Wal-Mart, and its mini-fridges are tailor-made for their space-constrained dorm rooms. (Many of them think that it is perhaps a German brand and Haier is not keen to disabuse them of the misperception.) The "good enough" effect is also one of the main reasons for the spectacular rise in the fortunes of private labels or store brands, vis-à-vis national brands, in supermarkets all across the world. Not only do these items provide the same or even better performance than the brand name products (in Europe, tests have shown that Aldi soap powder is at least as good as those made by P&G and Unilever – in some cases, the Aldi products work even better), lately, their design and packaging have vastly improved as well.

3. *Role of the Internet*: The above factor has been assisted by the various customer-centric websites that are plentiful on the Internet and also within individual blogs (or online diaries). The latter provide relatively reliable, albeit subjective, information that can help in consumer decision-making. These sites often supply information about products with unfamiliar brand names, such as those made in Asia but which are basically comparable in quality to the better-known established brands. Customer-oriented sites on the Internet also provide plenty of price and

feature-related information to allow for a detailed comparison of the offers from multiple dealers and retailers. People are thus able to judge for themselves if the available discount versions are good enough for them. This added benefit tends to work against the prospects of the middle-tier firms and their previously unchallenged ability to charge higher margins.

4. *The two-class syndrome*: At a more macro-level, what is presently taking place in the markets is a mirror image of the broader societal divisions that have been forming in most developed countries for quite some time. That is resulting in essentially two social classes. Importantly, the class divisions go beyond the usual distinctions that are made on wealth and income. Instead, the classes can now be distinguished by a disparate selection of demographic and psychographic criteria – education, cultural affinity, trust in institutions, hobbies and interests, and so on. As a result, there is today one consumer who seeks entertainment from the popular shows on television, and another who does not watch TV at all but goes to the opera; one who seeks out the cheaper food deals from a discount supermarket, and the other who avoids GM food like the plague, and buys the organic labels exclusively. Such a polarizing trend is clearly detrimental to the interests of the middle-market firms.

5. *Hybrid shopping patterns*: If possession of luxury objects once demarcated the social classes, this is no longer the case today. More and more consumers are shopping for brands that may seem to an independent observer as being beyond the reach of their purses. It is a classic and universal modern-day phenomenon. Women working in humdrum secretarial jobs in Europe, Japan, and America are seen to go to work in Chanel suits. Teenagers limited to miniscule parental allowances routinely flaunt the latest in mobile phone and digital music technology. Low-income slums in Mumbai and Johannesburg are roofed with such a profusion of electronic antennae that they resemble the outer shell of a porcupine – evidence, of course, that these tenements are equipped with cutting-edge satellite television sets. The factors driving these consumption patterns are based partly on one's need to reward oneself for the daily grind of living – by owning a once-in-a-lifetime, aspiration product. This is also due to the widespread desire to emulate the lifestyles of the rich and famous, and by the brands themselves becoming more accessible through their introduction of cheaper versions. To some extent, many middle-income shoppers have adopted certain brands as their own, individual talismans – of material success and sense gratification. Burberry in Britain, Louis Vuitton in Japan, Mercedes in the United States, and Japanese and Korean electronics brands in the developing world have especially benefited

from this development. This has led to a situation whereby brands are suddenly appearing in combinations that previously would have been unthinkable. We now have the phenomenon of a mother who drives to a Wal-Mart for her weekly shopping in her Mercedes, or a teenaged girl who matches a Louis Vuitton handbag with her H&M dress. Marketers and sociologists have labeled this trend as "the rise of the hybrid consumer". Once again, this development militates against the prospects of middle-market brands.

6. *Growing financial clout of the single woman*: It has often been said, with considerable truth, that the financial fortunes of the European luxury houses rise and fall resting squarely on the shopping behavior of the young, single Japanese woman. For many years, the latter's buying habits and fetishes have resulted in tremendous profits for firms like Louis Vuitton, Gucci, Chanel, and Prada. The LV bag is still considered *de rigueur* for Tokyo women for use in their offices and at family parties. Lately, single, working women from other countries, notably the U.S., Russia, China and India, have taken on a similar role. These women are becoming increasingly affluent and thereby independent in their purchase decisions. Now, they are seeking out their pet luxury brands of clothes and accessories to supplement their lifestyles. No doubt, the upsurge in luxury buying that one sees today is largely accounted for by this factor.

7. *Over-marketing*: As we have discussed in Chapter 2, many once-respected middle-tier brands have damaged their own reputations through a series of over-zealous and questionable marketing decisions that can only be called over-marketing. These brands previously stood for certain standard values in the eyes of the consumer and communicated a clear, middle-of-the-road image. But that increasingly has become vague and blurred because they are now seen as being too available, too imitating of others, and too eager to make profits – violating all of the essential pull marketing precepts. The perception which most people have derived is that these brands no longer provide any substantial difference relative to their less expensive (discounter) rivals, since both practice similar sales strategies. So, they have flocked to buying the cheaper ones instead. As a result, those tired old brands of yesteryears often do not count when the discerning buyers of today are looking for either something top-notch and exciting or something cheap and functional.

How can firms cope in this evolving market scenario?

The prospect of being "caught in the middle" between a 500-pound, gorilla-like Wal-Mart at one end and a nimble and feral cheetah-like Ferrari at the other can be a daunting one indeed for a mass-market, middle-tier firm. Where does the future lie? It is becoming increasingly obvious that many of these companies and brands will probably not survive the onslaught simply because they cannot match the efficiencies that a Wal-Mart, Tesco, Ryanair, or Southwest has, nor can they achieve the image and status of a Ferrari or Porsche overnight. The jury is therefore clearly out for the bankruptcy-ridden U.S. airline carriers like United, USAir, and Delta, and the ailing ones like Alitalia, JAL, and Swiss.

On the other hand, it may be too early to write the obituaries of some of these firms. Already, the clever and the ingenious among them have found a way of coping with the problems and a few are even thriving. Their strategy has evolved through finding a suitable market space where they can manage a toehold. In a market where a Wal-Mart or its equivalent dominates the low-end and a Ferrari-like competitor reigns at the high-end, firms in the middle are still not bereft of certain "zones" or niches, where they may actually end up doing very well if they are well-positioned there and execute the right plan. For the sake of descriptiveness, let us call these zones the market's "sweet spots".

The two sweet spots

"The Target (or equivalently, H&M, Zara, or Skoda) zone"

The rationale for this attractive and potentially profitable market space at the market's lower end is the opportunity to execute better than the hard discounters, since even their low prices can become tiresome to some people after a while. Some buyers can be put off by the lack of variety, the predictable nature of the offerings, and the pitiable level of service. Consider the following examples. Passengers on some of the discount airlines often complain about the mad dash that occurs to occupy the better seats and the noticeable lack of cleanliness inside the aircrafts themselves. Customers at some discount shops bemoan the absence of variety and selection in the offerings, as well as the unavailability of well-known brands. Some patrons of the discount segment in service categories (like banks and financial services) criticize the growing trend that they are unable to speak to anyone personally if they have a problem.

This gives rise to what we call the "Target Zone". In the U.S., where many retailers are taking a beating by the sheer size and clockwork efficiency of a popular discounter like Wal-Mart, the retailer Target has managed to hold its own and grow faster than even Wal-Mart itself. This the firm achieves by offering customers better quality products and more dedicated service, while still remaining competitive on the price aspect. Shoppers know that at a Target store they will not get the same bargain-basement prices that they could avail of at a hard discounter, but that there are much more attractive clothes, toys, appliances, and other items on offer. In other words, whereas the discounters compete mostly on the basis of providing "hard" or basic quality to their customers, Target has managed to introduce an element of soft or design quality – that critical "wow factor", which tips the scales in its favor. Then, the tradeoff between price and quality, which shoppers constantly make, becomes worthwhile and appealing to them. Target has been executing this strategy so well that even the managers of Wal-Mart have lately sought to improve the soft quality of their offerings.

What we call the Target zone can equivalently be described as the Skoda, H&M, Zara, or Virgin zone as well. In Europe, Volkswagen took a decrepit East European car factory making the rusty, but once-respected, Skoda cars and turned it around with precision German engineering. The result now is that Skoda cars, which sell cheaply, are better-looking and more reliable than their prices would warrant. In the apparel category, the Swedish Hennes & Mauritz and the Spanish Zara have played up the same philosophy of *cheap chic* to a hilt. Young women all over the world love their inexpensive fast-fashion clothes, which appear on the stores' racks as soon as a certain trend catches on. Finally, in the airline sector, Virgin Atlantic has won plaudits for providing its passengers with superior service and on-board amenities, while not overcharging on fares. Therefore, to sum up, in nearly all consumer industries something like a Target or a Skoda that offers some level of excitement, trendiness, and glitter, while remaining price-competitive at the same time, has a winning formula on its hands.

"The Coach (or BMW 3 Series) zone"

There is clearly a market for entry-level luxury, something that the luxury brands themselves know, but which (understandably) causes them to dither about introducing cheaper variants. Coach, the American leather goods brand, has fared very well in countries like Japan and the U.S., selling top-quality accessories like bags and shoes at sub-luxury prices. This is the space just below the premium luxury area, which implies high quality and engaging designs, but at prices that are not inaccessible to the average buyer. However, to execute in this space is potentially fraught with risk and the unthinkable prospect of causing damage to the valued mystique of a luxury brand. BMW, however, has managed to pull this tactic off successfully over the years with its dependable 3 Series. It has not caused any undue loss of prestige to the flagship 5 Series and the premium 7 Series. But BMW's recent decisions to introduce a 1 Series and to relaunch the once-retired 6 Series are questionable at best, since these new versions seem destined to confuse the buyers and blur the time-tested brand logic. Similarly, Lexus, which had made its name and business in America by exploiting the "affordable luxury" aspect, then overreached itself by introducing a plethora of confusing, low-end versions.

Montblanc, the traditional German maker of top-quality writing equipments, too has been mindful of this dilemma of maintaining its image as a luxury product on the one hand and of catering to the less-affluent buyer on the other. Recently, it has introduced a more moderately priced range of ballpoint pens under the same Montblanc label. A worrying development, however, is the brand's expansion into many other unrelated products: perfumes, watches, and so on, a common pitfall of many a luxury brand.

Figure 3.1 illustrates the development of the marketing game, as discussed in the above sections. Firms in both of the sweet spots attempt to outdo their much stronger rivals that are positioned in an adjacent market space. From our discussion, it is not a given if they will manage to pull it off successfully over the long run. It all depends on the commitment and tenacity of their managers and their ability to exploit the mistakes of their dominant competitors.

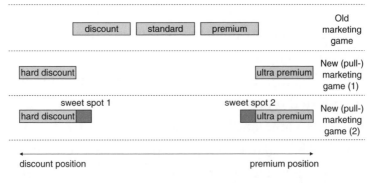

Figure 3.1   Development of the new marketing game

Market polarity and reverse psychology

Against the background of the trends and developments discussed above, we are forced to ask this question: is it a wise course for a firm to aspire to one of the two market "extremes", that is to be either a Wal-Mart or a Ferrari? If it does purport to be a wise strategy, we must again ask whether it is sufficient to be "extreme" in one single criterion, for example, price, in order to attain one of the two polarities. What really underlies these tactics from the point of view of reverse psychology marketing?

The answer to at least some of these questions is the imperative dictated by the present economic and societal dynamics. A Wal-Mart is a Wal-Mart, ferociously battling to reduce costs, strong-arming suppliers, and laying down rules for customers, only because the market inherently demands so. Buyers *are* happy with the lower prices they have to pay at the checkout aisles; they appear less sensitive to the facts that the hard discounters do not give them due attention and service; or that they have made many mom-and-pop stores to go out of business; or that they are causing job losses and uprooting entire communities. Most people seem unmindful of these issues and seem ready to forgive the successful market players. Even, Wal-Mart and Tesco's decisions to screen the music and video titles they sell are lauded by some consumer groups as a good way to protect children and teenagers from being exposed to their "pernicious" influence. Hence, a belief in the virtue of a "nanny marketer" is at work here – that somehow a paternalistic corporate entity is preferable to the complex choices of the market jungle.

The second reason why firms are opting for the two extremes is that the tools for executing them are more available in the present day than they ever were before. The opportunity to source production from low-wage countries, which is commonplace in these times, means that the hard discounters can translate it as an end-benefit to their customers. If they did not offer it, someone else would. Likewise, at the luxury end of the market, society has never been more enamored of the Hollywood actors, athletic celebrities, and assorted "stars". And the desire to mimic their lifestyles, behavior, and shopping choices has never been more pronounced. Consequently, luxury firms find it quite facile to sell an "attainable dream" to their clients by tying a certain premium offering like perfume, bag, or shoe, with the glamour and pulling power of a celebrity brand ambassador.

If we consider the strategies of the hard discounters and the premium luxury brands in the aggregate, we are struck by a strange commonality in their underlying philosophies. They both practice "anti-marketing" and reverse psychology marketing tactics to the core! The discounters do it because they have to, in order to save costs. The luxury brands do it for a different reason – because they should. If they stoop to the level of the other brands, they are then seen to have cheapened their status and mystique. Looking at the discounters' position, we find many aspects of the "less" strategy (more on this in Chapter 6). Traditional marketing calls for more: more stores, more choices, more availability, and so on. In contrast, the discounters manage to sell "less" – less product availability, fewer choices, and little service, all suggestive of reverse psychology. These companies decide for themselves what is good for the customer, and then proceed to offer it on a "Take it or leave it" basis.

The picture is similar in principle but different in practice at the other end of the scale, in the premium luxury segment. Here, too, products are not always developed first and foremost with the customer in mind. Whereas the discounters start with cost as the chief criterion, for luxury products it is the idiosyncratic mark of the creator and designer that has to be stamped first. Frequently, their main objective is to be seen as leading the pack or setting a trend. This is particularly true of the major fashion houses and luxury groups. Often, the couture and designs emanating from their catwalks are so outré and shocking that they are considered hardly suitable for the average customer. But, as is widely known, the shows and events generate the publicity and buzz, while the more traditional and generally accepted patterns are sold in the boutiques. In broad terms, however, manufacturers of luxury goods are said to make them "for their own sake", much like the craft of an artist or a creative genius. Those customers

who are then prepared to pay the price accept a cor-
respondingly long waiting time for delivery, as for a
Ferrari. Hence, strategies that are symbolic of reverse
psychology and anti-marketing can be found in both
the discount and the luxury segments.

4

Network buzz and pull

Those of us who follow the fortunes of business, media, and popular culture frequently hear expressions of awe and wonder at the scale of successes and failures today. Nowadays, a product, book, film, music group, or celebrity that is acclaimed to be a hit is not merely a modest success but often *grandiosely* so. Conversely, failures are no longer "passable" failures as in the old days, but usually abject and abysmal flops. Coke C2 (two-calorie cola) was such a flop – it barely registered a ripple on the sea of new products that are launched each year. In contrast, consider the blockbuster success of the Apple iPod, the Dyson vacuum cleaner, *The Da Vinci Code*, the *Arctic Monkeys* rock group, or the *Harry Potter* series. It is reported that the iPod has an unbelievable 75 percent market share in the MP3 player market – this despite the existence of several worthy competing brands that offer the same or better functionality at a much cheaper price. *The Da Vinci Code* reportedly has sold 40 million copies worldwide as well as being translated into dozens of foreign languages! Why does a teenager feel that he or she must own *only* the iPod? How could an anonymous bunch of teenagers from Sheffield, U.K. with the incongruous name *Arctic Monkeys* become an overnight music phenomenon? Why is it that the joke goes that one is not allowed through airport check-in around the globe if one does not carry *The Da Vinci Code* on one's person? Why do parents worldwide feel oppressed about what they have to do whenever the latest Harry Potter book or movie comes along?

To answer all such questions, one has to address the growing power of buyer networks these days. In truth, networks have existed in history ever since people began to interact socially, and commerce and trade have long made use of them knowingly or unknowingly. The reputation of Chinese silk, Indian muslin, and Japanese woodblocks was disseminated far into the innermost reaches of continental Europe even during the Dark Ages. Travelers along the well-trodden trade routes would share stories about the respective merits of items from various countries. Shrewd merchants understood the boost that the patronage of royalty or the nobility could give their goods in hawking them to the broader mass of commoners. British shopkeepers like Fortnum & Mason still display their royal warrants outside the stores. But, what has changed now is in the *scale*. Whereas a network of people in a town or region could sway a new offering one way or another, toward a marginal profitability or marginal loss, in these days the tide operates on a global level, with repercussions that are no longer marginal but huge. The cliché is worth repeating that people are more connected than they ever were, thanks to the ready availability and use of mobile phones and the Internet. What this means in business terms is that word-of-mouth or "buzz", which is the true arbiter of a new product, operates today worldwide and near-instantly. Ten years ago, it was not hard for a Hollywood movie that flopped in the U.S. to get a second lease on life from runs in theaters in Europe or Asia. It is well near impossible to achieve that today. Negative feedback will spread to distant countries from sites and blogs on the Internet, marring whatever chance of success the film may have had previously. In fact, because of this risk, some movie studios have renounced the lagged rollout they once did of their films in other countries based on their commercial importance. Also, on the positive side, the clamor to view a hit movie at the same time as the American audience is just too great, because moviegoers in those places have already been primed to watch it from the buzz circulating on the web. There is a perverse reason as well – to deny poachers in those other countries the opportunity to make money from screening bootlegged versions. They all make the same point about global inter-connectedness.

Globalization, that is the idea that a homegrown business can spread its wings and serve the farthest reaches of the globe with a minimum of tariffs and regulations, has many vocal champions and detractors. Its proponents see the virtues from better products and higher living standards in the far-off places, and more jobs, profits, and shareholder wealth at home. Its critics, on the other hand, bemoan the loss of indigenous cultures, community values, dietary habits, and traditional livelihoods in the face of an overpowering corporation with its seductive marketing and its "one size fits all" model. Notwithstanding the criticisms, the fact is that nothing can halt the wheels of globalization; the present time and contemporary society demand it. And already there are some unexpected and astonishing results. Beyond the stereotypical examples of Mongolian and Uzbek teenagers watching MTV or women under purdah following the saucy episodes of *Baywatch*, a fascinating and much-less-publicized phenomenon is unfolding among the less-sophisticated populaces of the world. News emerged from India that in its so-called "cow-belt", that is the country's impoverished northern states, Hindi translations of American business and personal development titles are local bestsellers. *Rich Dad – Poor Dad, Who Moved My Cheese, Seven Habits of Highly Effective People*, and *Questions are the Answers* are very popular among the rural youth, as they seek to improve their lives and the breadth of their thinking. The really interesting aspect of this development is that these young people, who are presumed to live in a backward region, are not content with the ideas emanating from local authors in Delhi or Mumbai, as their parents may have done before. But, they feel the need to stay abreast of the latest Western thinking. Clearly, the notion of the entire world being on the same page presents businesses with tremendous, far-reaching, but as-yet-unforeseen prospects.

Perhaps, in this context one can mention a couple of descriptive anecdotes. In one of her talk shows, Oprah Winfrey, the American media celebrity, had a little destitute girl on her lap in a remote impoverished area of South Africa. The little girl said that she did not know who Oprah was, but when told that she had come from America she eagerly wanted to know if she knew Britney Spears.

More recently, the chairman of Microsoft and world's richest man Bill Gates made a whistle-stop tour of Vietnam. What took him by complete bewilderment and surprise was the rousing, heartfelt reception he got everywhere from this one-time enemy of the U.S. He was feted and welcomed at every event as a world-conquering hero. News-reports said that tens of thousands of young Vietnamese came to see him and to hear him talk, with many clutching Vietnamese editions of his authored books.

Opportunities and challenges from a networked society

This rising level of global inter-connectedness presents significant opportunities and challenges to marketers. One major opportunity is to rapidly build a network of clients without incurring significant start-up costs through traditional advertising, branding, and sales promotions that were necessary before.

With the right product and costs under control, business seems to take off on its own. Word-of-mouth or buzz is, of course, the ally here and the Internet is its ideal conduit. And now it is easier to expand a successful enterprise by crossing regional and country-specific boundaries because word-of-mouth has preceded to ready the foreign markets for the new product. Consider AC Hotels, a Spanish hotel chain that was founded only in 1998, and that is expanding at a fast pace throughout western Europe. It already has 62 hotels with 30 more in planning, some in the U.S. It offers all modern amenities, trendy *avant-garde* design, and the latest in technology (e.g., free Internet access) – in short, everything that a busy tourist or business traveler would need, but without the unnecessary extras, all at a reasonable rate. The enthusiastic response it has had from its guests and the glowing reviews it has received in the European press have created a cult-like subculture. People dwell on the distinctive details of staying at an AC hotel, such as having four pillows on the bed, free newspapers, and free round-the-clock refreshments and snacks, which usually mean that they seek out one whenever they travel. Hence, what started as a small-scale success story known only to the regional Spanish has grown rapidly being embraced by the other Europeans.

The younger people of today are much more product-oriented and far less susceptible to marketing gimmicks and extravagant ad claims than the previous generations. In fact, they could be called the prototypical "show me" generation. The idea of reverse psychology works well on them since they are intrigued, even enthralled, by any "unexpected" tactics from firms, whom they generally take to be self-serving and profit-oriented. The two European apparel chains, the Spanish Zara and the Swedish H&M, are playing this game with considerable panache. Their stylish, fashion-forward clothes at prices that do not seem to match lead to that initial, quizzical interest among young women – the desire to come, see, and judge for themselves if the deal is worthwhile – and, finally, that internally resounding "wow" once the matter is settled beyond doubt. Not surprisingly, these stores have substantial pulling power over their customers, and their rivals have, accordingly, copied the strategy wholesale.

The moral for all companies is that they have to work on their product and brand superiority, price them reasonably, focus less on glitzy campaigns, and attempt to *pull* customers instead. The key, above all, lies in building a viable customer network by recruiting or giving incentives to certain influential members (whom we call "hubs"), who will bring their followers in their wake (more on this later). The up-and-coming Korean firms like Samsung and LG understand this new market picture well. They are extremely product-focused, like the Japanese companies of yesteryears. Both Samsung and LG have managed to capture the imaginations of the world's youth with their trendy yet affordable mobile phones, and those of their parents with the latest generation of flat-panel TVs. But what is more important is that the Korean companies have become very adept at recruiting local celebrities in different countries to make their brands more visible (and liked) and to garner a larger following. Consider the case of Samsung in India. From a virtually unknown quantity in 1995, it now has an awareness level close to 100 percent and is one of the most admired brands in the country. To do this, Samsung chose the right touchstones of this billion-customer market. The company associated itself with the two major obsessions of average Indians: cricket and Bollywood films. Samsung sponsored the eagerly followed India–Pakistan cricket series and an annual Film award. Consequently, its sales of mobile phones, TVs, microwave ovens, and washing machines have catapulted recently, and the firm now finds itself as one of the most trusted brands of the Indian middle class.

Sometimes, a business can rapidly build a network without having to champion an event or seeking a celebrity's endorsement, but by doing something quite straightforward. It can just create a "buyer prototype" that most people can relate to – a *customer clone*, as it were. This simple yet powerful recipe is behind the amazing rise of the easyGroup businesses that are mushrooming throughout Europe. They started from easyJet, the discount airline founded in 1995 by the Cypriot-born Stelios Haji-Ioannou, and now include some 20 assorted operations like easyCruise, easyBus, easyCar, easyMobile, easyHotel, and even easyPizza. What accounts for such a speedy ramp-up of businesses across disparate industries within 10 years? The answer is the same as what Sir Richard Branson had done before with his Virgin label. easyJet effectively created its network *by inventing the easyCustomer*. He is the archetypal social underdog, who believes in the brand's stated credo of delivering value, keeping it simple, and taking on the big boys. The fact that most people understand and can relate to such a person has caused the network to extend so easily.

The Starbucks coffee-shop chain has been growing at an extraordinary pace within the U.S. and in the rest of the world by similarly benefiting from the virtuous effects of a network. There is also a prototypical "Starbucks customer". It does not take long to figure out the profile when one enters a Starbucks shop anywhere in the world. He or she, and more often it is a she, is young, well-educated, and upwardly mobile, for whom a cup of good coffee is as much an expression of her culture and sophistication as it is a reviving potion. Starbucks' critics in America express incredulity and wonder at how the chain can have such pulling power over its clients, who show up religiously each day and overpay for a cup of coffee when they could have one of the same quality at chains like Dunkin' Donuts and Wawa at a fraction of the cost. The reason for this is not the fine arabica beans that Starbucks uses or their reportedly high caffeine content that some researchers believe make people into Starbucks addicts. In our view, Starbucks performs the role of a social club. When its clients walk in or choose to linger there while nursing a cup of coffee, they are comforted and reassured to see people of a similar background all around them. From this perspective, there may be an element of truth to the jest heard in some quarters that Starbucks is actually a dating club masquerading as a coffee chain.

The challenge from a network, however, is in knowing how large it ought to be (i.e., when to stop) so that it is sustainable on the long run and has no adverse effects on quality, customer service, and brand mystique. As for Starbucks, there is already a sense that the firm may have overreached by expanding perhaps *too* much. In fact, the Starbucks network may have become too large for its own good. Just in the Times Square section of Manhattan there are now *four* Starbucks shops jostling for customer attention and traffic. Through its over-expansion, Starbucks may indeed have made room for a *smaller*, but truly up-market chain in America, now that people have begun to appreciate the finer points of coffee. This has already happened in the U.K. where chains like Caffè Nero and Costa Coffee are winning the consumer accolades. Japan has had a parallel experience. It was the first foreign country that Starbucks ventured in and where it was hailed as an instant success. In the beginning, the company grew there at a frenetic pace, opening numerous out-lets and registering a high volume of sales. But then customer fatigue set in and what was seen before as a novelty like its "no smoking" policy, a rarity in a Japanese *kissaten* (coffee-shop), soon became an irksome constraint. It gave the established Japanese rival Doutor the opportunity to outflank Starbucks by launching a *more* upscale chain called Excelsior. This new shop claims to serve an even better quality of coffee and allows smoking in designated areas. So, Starbucks Japan now finds itself being squeezed in the middle between the upscale Excelsior on the one hand and the low-priced Doutor on the other, while its erstwhile "phenomenon" proceeds to level off. Customer networks, it should be understood, can act as a dual-edged sword.

The brand as a social network

The Starbucks example shows us how a brand ought to be viewed and understood today. The traditional branding ideas that were discussed in Chapter 2 are becoming increasingly obsolete to serve present-day business needs. Many firms today face the daunting test to reclaim the currency of their mature brands, which is under threat from the ineffectiveness of mass-media advertising, changing customer tastes, and the emergence of trendy yet low-cost competitors. Existing brand perspectives provide little solace and succor to these troubled managers. In this age of fast and furious product development and product obsolescence, complicated by the twin challenges of globalization and technology, businesses should take a fresh look at how they regard their own brands and what makes them compete better.

From the many examples cited throughout this book, if one considers the way successful companies are managing their brands and engaging in competition, a common theme emerges: *Brands are increasingly being defined in terms of the network of customers they "own" and inter-brand (and thus, inter-firm) rivalry is more often a test of which one is able to develop and retain a loyal and more profitable network.*

Those firms that are able to sustain a core network of buyers through their brands' pulling power are able to stay profitable even in troubled times when a sea of losses seems to swamp their rivals. Consider a few product successes from recent times. Red Bull, Apple, Ebay, Louis Vuitton, Jimmy Choo, Manolo Blahnik, H&M, Sean John, and Dolce & Gabbana, all share a common marketing story. It is the way each has won over devoted followers by creating and sustaining a social network of customers who have embraced the offerings. All of these brand networks exert considerable gravitational power on their customers. Indeed, their loyal followers believe in them to such an extent that, in many cases, they act as their unpaid word-of-mouth ambassadors. Not only do these so-called "customer evangelists" buy on their own, they manage to persuade their families and friends to buy as well – perpetuating the network principle. We thus have teenagers for whom nothing other than the iPod will do, because through possessing one they connect with their friends at home as well as with peers around the world. In our own experience, we also understood that a similar phenomenon was taking place when we heard from friends, colleagues, and family members unsolicited suggestions to read *The Da Vinci Code*. Something like this had never happened to us before.

A brand network that is strong also provides adequate defense against competitors' attempting to wean customers away from it. This explains why the Coca-Cola Company, despite the vaunted marketing and financial muscle, has been unable to dent the popularity of Red Bull from pushing its own energy drink Full Throttle to young adults. For youth globally, Red Bull is the axiomatic choice – the standard in energy drinks. Red Bull has truly made a business out of network building. To such an extent that its presumed effects on enhancing stamina and mental alertness have now entered the collective youth consciousness, and "vodka and Red Bull" is very much part of the cultural lexicon. Coke's Full Throttle does not quite pass that buzz test. Another global marketing powerhouse, Anheuser-Busch, has had a similarly frustrating experience with its own Mexican beer version Tequiza. For years it has been struggling to catch up with America's number one brand of imported beer – Grupo Mondelo's Corona Extra.

These examples show that when there is an incumbent brand with an associated strong and loyal customer network it is not at all easy to supplant it, notwithstanding whatever marketing prowess and financial backing may be at hand. Thus, Yahoo auctions has not had much of an impact against Ebay in America. For Ebay, the sum total of its business *is* its community – the 150-million-strong network of small-time buyers and mom-and-pop auctioneers who represent the lifeblood of its business, and its number one asset. Ironically, Ebay has encountered similar problems trying to displace Taobao, the number one auction site in China. The latter's network is much larger than Ebay's and its free bidding offer is a far more attractive proposition to Chinese web-auction fans.

There is another dynamic at work here. In many industries, especially those where there is an implicit technology or product-based standard, firms that are able to cobble together a critical mass of customers *first* benefit from a positive feedback mechanism. A bandwagon phenomenon ensues. The firm's initial success in winning over customers leads to even greater success – which allows these firms to corner the market eventually. This effect is frequently seen in network-based industries, such as online auction sites and mobile phone services. This is also how many Microsoft products, like Word, Excel, and Explorer, came to dominate their markets. Economists call these effects "network externalities" but most people understand this as the power of large networks.

But there is a countervailing aspect as well to keep businesses true. When networks grow in size and scale, other factors like quality control, customer service, brand image, and managerial focus enter the picture. Since any brand network operates rather like a social club, when more and more members join, the existing members may find that the quality has deteriorated and service is not what it used to be. Some may start to believe that the club is giving short shrift to existing members and is solely interested in getting new ones by giving them better incentives to join. Then, the old members feel neglected and start defecting to a smaller and more client-friendly network. Incidentally, this factor is behind the steady rise of the consumer-oriented, good neighbor-like Commerce Bank in the U.S. This bank has made it a mission to cater to customers who feel they have been underserved by the large, faceless conglomerates, which, they believe, are more interested in size and profits. Commerce Bank plays up the act of a small, local bank, even though it is not really small or local. It stays open all week, keeps long hours, and calls itself "America's most convenient bank". The key lesson for brand networks that have grown large is therefore learning how to "act small".

When a firm starts thinking of its brands in terms of their customer networks it can make better strategic choices. Some years back, Merrill Lynch's brokerage division made a tactical choice to retreat from the business of small investors, handing them over to Schwab, E-Trade, and other low-commission brokers. Merrill chose to focus instead on serving individuals with higher net-worths and investment portfolios. In hindsight, this customer-selection

strategy has paid off well for Merrill since it effectively "homogenized" the customer network, which
became smaller but also *tighter* (i.e., more loyal
to the firm), more manageable, and less churn-
prone. The present network of Merrill customers is
driven less by the size of commissions but more
by the products, service, and advice that the company offers. Similarly, banks that issue credit cards
have found that their traditional branding and mass-
mailing approaches do not deliver the promised
flow of new cardholders. Instead, they have had
more benefit from linking up with various social
and professional organizations that consist of tight
and committed networks of like-minded individuals,
like the World Wildlife Fund, American Association
of Retired Persons (AARP), and various university
alumni groups. This has led to the creation of the
so-called "affinity cards", which provide far better
returns to credit card firms. This example shows that
when it is difficult to start a new brand network, it
is more effective to tie up with an existing one.

Networks are now playing a very important role during the buying and selling of brands, business units,
and entire companies. The major strategic objective underlying most corporate buy-outs and brand
acquisitions is the expectation on the part of the
acquiring firm that it stands to appropriate the customer network of the acquired firm or brand. In
fact, the financial valuation of brands during M&A
(mergers and acquisitions) activity is increasingly
being based on their customer franchises. Microsoft

paid a hefty $385 million to the two young founders of the free email service Hotmail because it saw the prospect of corralling Hotmail's 10-million-strong user network into the folds of its MSN portal. The online auction site Ebay also wanted to co-opt the growing, cult-like following of Half.com by acquiring the site and by weaning its buyers into the Ebay community.

Explaining cult brands

This is the right juncture to discuss the idea of a cult brand, and to attempt to explain the magical spell it manages to cast on its adherents, be it for only a short time. One can better understand the dynamics, tactics, rewards, and potential of the reverse psychology strategy from taking a closer look at these rather special brands. The term "cult brand", however, is perhaps the least understood and most misused one in marketing. In reality, it is a *very successful instance* of a brand's social network in that it has a very strong and dedicated buyer following. Here, the brand usually stands for certain higher meanings and values to a relatively small but tightly linked group of extremely passionate customers, who become attached to it into something resembling a minor religion. Fans of Leica cameras, A. Lange and Söhne watches, Harley-Davidson motorcycles, Krug champagne, and Bottega Veneta bags display the classic traits of a cult-like subculture. It is built on a shared purchase and consumption experience with the brand at the center. By definition, a cult brand starts out small and remains hidden for a time from the mainstream media and culture, as if to exert its subterranean and mysterious "hold" on its initial adherents. The network grows organically as new customers are pulled into it by virtue of buzz and hearsay alone. Meanwhile, the brand sedulously avoids both unabashed commercialism and the glare of media publicity.

Cult brands teach us interesting and valuable lessons about the power of reverse psychology marketing. All of the qualities discussed in the above paragraph have been seen contributing to the behind-the-scenes success of the Japanese cult apparel brand called BAPE. Its founder Nigo (or "number two") is famous for shunning the limelight and has been quoted as saying that he does not want a lot of people wearing his clothes. He tells celebrities who buy the brand *not* to flaunt the connection to the media. He does not advertise the locations of his stores, which are intentionally unmarked, and even limits the number of items his buyers can have. All the same, BAPE has become a rage among young people, and when its first and only store in America opened in the Soho district of New York there were waiting lines to get in.

There is a somewhat similar story presently unfolding in malls across America that have seen a new chain of stores called *Hot Topic*. From the outside it looks like any other youth clothing store but unknown to most adults, its appeal lies in the fact that it sells to the devoted and growing following of teens who call themselves "Goths". One sees them in cities across America, Europe, and Asia, dressed exclusively in black with various black appendages (hair, mascara, jewelry, etc.) and rallying to the music of the *Grateful Dead*. Some mistake them for being followers of some abstruse, occult ideology but most Goths tend to be well-meaning young people who claim they are merely expressing their individualities.

It goes without saying, of course, that cult brands have considerable pulling power over many people. Their appeal usually springs from their offerings, their patiently staked reputation for quality and work-manship, and their obvious dedication to their trade as though it were a higher calling. Some seem to display an inexplicable aloofness to success, sym-bolic of a *genuine* reverse psychology mindset, as if to convey a certain disdain for sales and profits. The message is usually "We are not really interested in profit for profit's sake". Consider the following instances. Ferrari caps its production between 2500 and 3000 cars a year, has waiting lists in the U.S. and Japan, when it could conceivably make and sell a lot more. Krug goes to extreme lengths to produce a superior champagne to merit the status of a *Grande Cuvée*, even if that means having to age the wine 6–8 years in traditionally small, oak barrels. It has often been observed, with a touch of irony, that the Porsche is a small, expensive, and impractical car. Its mystique among car fanatics, however, derives from its fastidious product-oriented philosophy – as the ultimate car-lover's car – defying the concept of annual model changes practiced by other car-makers. Porsche imperiously sticks to only a few, time-tested versions over time. The *Dave Matthews* band also has a cult-like appeal among music lovers, especially among young college students. The band regularly makes one of the highest-grossing concert tours annually. Although their music is not played often on radio, their shows always sell out quickly. Part of their drawing power is the group's vocal support for environmental and earthly friendly causes. But, more noteworthy perhaps is that, in contrast to the other shows, the Dave Matthews band actually allows, *even encourages*, "bootlegging" by their fans and actually facilitates them to record the live concerts.

Generally speaking, many cult brands are world-famous luxury brands because they are made with such a finicky attention to detail and so few of them are produced and distributed. But they do not always have to be. In fact, the best examples of cult brands are those that belong to everyday product categories and are unfamiliar to the broader global audience, justifying the cult appellation. This is in marked contrast to something like a Harley-Davidson, which is widely known, publicized, and marketed as a cult brand. In fact, the true and archetypal cult brand should only be known *within* a sub-population, which therefore becomes tightly linked to the brand and sustains its business.

Such an example is Manner, the tasty wafer-biscuit that has long acted as a much beloved symbol within the small country of Austria. The appeal of Manner among Austrians derives from its long history, its distinctive pink packaging, its continuous family-operated business, and the local people's nostalgic memories of their childhood when Manner biscuits played a cherished role. Indeed, in one of his films Arnold Schwarzenegger, a native Austrian, lent subtle patronage to Manner, but which largely went unnoticed by the larger world audience. In a scene from the hit *Terminator* movie, Arnold's robotic self is seen to casually pick up a Manner biscuit at a convenience store. The gesture was happily picked up by all Austrians. Likewise, in Austria the famed *Hotel Sacher* and its eponymous coffee shops have a cult-like quality that draw their allure from the genteel, old-world Viennese charm and, of course, from the Sacher-Torte, the most famous cake in the world. The latter was known to be the favorite dessert of Austrian archdukes and empresses. Historical links and anecdotes, such as these, usually enhance the charm and mystique of a cult brand, and keep it alive for many generations.

But cult brands do not need to have such an exalted parentage – they can have very humble origins, and still merit the cult appellation. In Philadelphia there is such a small, family-owned shop in the rundown northern part of the city where it sells bagels, salads, and sandwiches mostly to university students. The food has a cult following among repeat buyers, who are usually seen standing in long lines even in the cold and rain. The owners, a husband-and-wife couple, are frequently seen arguing in front of the customers. But, it only adds to the charm. In fact, the devoted customer-base gloss over other such minor details that the store has a limited menu or that it charges more for nearly everything!

The pulling power of cult brands

It is not really hard to understand the pulling power of cult brands. The message they send to consumers is refreshingly different from the attention seek-ing, usually loud, self-aggrandizing claims of push-marketers. The symbolic hauteur that cult brands generally possess and their seeming disinterestedness in mundane financial benefits combine to make them all the more alluring to the average buyer. This is of course true if their core offering is considered worth having. Here, interestingly, the nature of the offering is often dictated at the behest of the seller, not the buyer. A cult restaurant may open on an irregular schedule and serve food that is "chef's choice", that is beyond the decision-making power of the clien-tele. From this perspective, some cult brands may be said to practice "anti-marketing" tactics (see details in Chapter 6), in that they do not go out of their way to bring attention to themselves nor do they seek to overly cater to customers' desires. Yet, customers still flock in droves.

As the customer network of such an enterprise grows over time, it naturally tends to diminish its cult aspect. The onus on its managers is then to stay true to the set of values that created the network in the first place and to reaffirm them to the clientele. That is only if the brand wishes to remain a cult. Some may find that their newfound popularity and ensuing profits are more than acceptable and the brand chooses to become more mainstream and commercial. Volkswagen went in that direction with its Beetle car, which was once associated with hippies. Indeed, it was probably not correct to describe the Beetle as the "world's largest selling cult brand" after having sold 21 million of them in its history! Likewise, although Apple is often mentioned as a cult brand, we are skeptical if its more recent customers really care about the values that company has been known to espouse, but are merely interested in getting hold of the desirable iPod. Indeed, post-iPod Apple no longer has the same underdog (anti-Wintel, "Think Different", etc.) quality, and its recent attempts to present a more conventional and mainstream image will undoubtedly detract from the cult appeal of its past.

Here, a caveat is in order. While some firms can safely make the transition from cult to mainstream, history tells us that most end up as failures. Indeed, cult brands that overtly stray from the values that built their customer networks end up paying a heavy price. Their core customers, the ones who propagate the network, are fiercely protective of what they see to be the intrinsic principles that identify the brand and even define *themselves* from those ideas. If the firm is seen to have become blatantly profit-seeking or too commercial, they suffer a sense of betrayal, a symbolic loss of identity, and a feeling that something precious has been given up. And the resulting backlash can hurt the brand irrevocably.

The rise and fall of Snapple is a classic story that illustrates the qualities that make for a successful cult brand and the marketing missteps that damage it. Founded by three blue-collar New Yorkers, Snapple iced tea and fruit juices once had a quirky cult-like subculture in the U.S. Its charm lay in the healthy, new age, and eco-friendly quality of the drinks that also derived from the slogan: "Made from the best stuff on earth". Moreover, the firm's unsophisticated, somewhat amateurish television commercials featuring "Wendy, the Snapple Lady", who was Wendy Kaufman, an actual Snapple employee, were very popular with the general public. These advertisements generated a lot of publicity and buzz. The Snapple customer network, however, was small and regionally concentrated. Nonetheless, this base was very loyal and profitable. Then, Quaker Oats, a much larger company, acquired Snapple and proceeded to replace the quirky, regional image with a slick branding campaign to appeal to the larger national market. Wendy, the Snapple Lady, was summarily dropped. The distribution channels were changed from convenience stores to supermarkets and even the traditionally small bottles of Snapple were made larger. Not unexpectedly, the whole strategy back-fired. Those Snapple buyers who liked its homely, noncommercial quality felt betrayed by the change of image and lost interest in the brand altogether. The mystique that Snapple had before was lost forever.

The British luxury firm Burberry has been fever-ishly attempting to preserve the cachet of its label in view of a different and not altogether unwelcome sort of problem – over-popularity. Recently, the firm underwent a remarkable revival of fortunes under the leadership of Rose Marie Bravo, an American retail executive, going from a drab, stodgy, and some-what passé English label to a stylish and up-market cult brand. Its distinctive, camel-plaid design quickly became a rage in Europe, America, and Asia showing up as must-have club-wear for young people. But, perhaps the popularity came a little too much and a little too soon. News got out that some of Burberry's traditionally affluent customers, that is those who pay for the more expensive clothes and accessories, were avoiding the label because it was becoming *too* visible. Its signature scarves and baseball caps had become the *de rigueur* uniform of the so-called British "*chavs*", lower-income sections of the popu-lace who want to copy the look and style of actors, models, and footballers' wives. Lately, Burberry has discontinued some clothing items and pruned the recognizable check design to only a small fraction of its product lineup.

The role of hubs in network creation

In a networked society such as ours, where two complete strangers are divided supposedly by only a few degrees of separation, it stands to reason that some of us should be more connected than others. Certain individuals are regarded as leaders of their *own* tight circles, as people to look up to, whose words and actions affect the thought and decisions of others. Such a person could be a respected family member, a popular friend, a learned teacher, or a wise mentor. At a somewhat broader level and in different cultures, there are also influential local politicians, community activists, religious figures, authors, musicians, newspaper columnists, society matrons, tribal chiefs, and village elders – all of whom exert some degree of influence over their loyal followers, masters, as it were, of their own little domains. At a far more extreme level, however, there are a few special people in every country, who are seemingly "connected" to nearly everyone of that country, and some even to the entire world. This is a David Beckham, an Oprah Winfrey, a Michael Jordan, an Angelina Jolie, a Britney Spears, a Tiger Woods, or a Mick Jagger. Their global celebrity and appeal could be said to have arisen from any number of factors – glamour, charisma, musical talent, acting ability, athletic prowess, and so on.

These rare individuals are the "hubs" of our networked society, the ones who have their own substantial private networks and who draw their followers metaphorically like a railway engine pulls compartments in its wake. The present age seems to be obsessed with such celebrities. People all over the world follow their daily lives, words, behaviors, shopping habits, and lifestyle and mate choices with an avidity that has never been known before – giving life, of course, to the vast number of gossip tabloids and society magazines. It is fair to say that these hubs have the ability to *sway* the decisions of large masses of people one way or the other, and if marketers were to tap that invaluable pulling power that these people possess, albeit for a time, they stand to gain a significant advantage.

David Beckham is an exceptional hub whose name and face are familiar to the global audience, rich and poor, young and old, male and (particularly) female. His feats as the erstwhile Manchester United and England football star, his good looks, marriage to one of the Spice girls, multi-million dollar transfer to Real Madrid, and a movie-theme (*Bend It Like Beckham*) have made him into an irresistible celebrity whose exploits on and off the field draw attention on a worldwide scale. The connection to football – the commoner's sport unlike tennis, golf, or cricket – is, of course, the key. Football is experiencing a worldwide resurgence of popularity, and the level of skill and competitiveness that is on display in the English and Spanish premier leagues is particularly compelling. And there have been few football players who have combined midfield generalship, dexterity with the freekick, *and* movie star looks as Beckham has.

Not surprisingly, his is the face that has been tapped for a large number of disparate products and services: sports shoes, soft drinks, mobile phone service, hair cream, colognes, and so on. It is a remarkable fact that his appeal is even stronger in Japan, where he could rightfully be called the most popular person, Japanese or otherwise, and his face stares from the walls of every subway station endorsing any given product.

From a reverse psychology standpoint, however, it is easy to get carried away by the fervor and hoopla surrounding David Beckham. He undoubtedly brings valuable attention to a business brand, and the positive attitudes that his fan-base has for him may even rub off on the products he endorses. But, that is true only to a point, and that too for a certain time. People can tire even of a modern-day athletic hero like Beckham. When they see him on a Vodafone poster one day and on an Adidas one the next, also in a Pepsi commercial, a Coty, and a Brylcreem – everything in the end becomes a blur. The question then arises in people's minds: "What does Beckham really stand for?" The answer could become something as fuzzy and hodge-podge as the corporate giant GE and its assorted disparate businesses that make certain business wags to quip that GE means "generally everything". Already, there are signs that Beckham's stock is on the wane. His recent on-field performance has been less than stellar and the move to Real Madrid has not materialized in the ideal way. The advice for both Beckham and his many sponsors is not to overdo the brand endorsements and to make a clear connection between the brands themselves and his basic persona.

Tiger Woods, the young American golf legend, also appears as the spokesperson and ambassador for a large number of well-known brands. However, the only one connection that works effectively in our view is his endorsement of the Tag Heuer watch. This logic is not hard to follow. There is a basic harmony and an innate commonality between the philosophy of the world-famous watch on the one hand and the world-famous golfer on the other. Both tend to push the proverbial envelope, stretching the limits set by man and nature, and both are associated with personal endurance and sporting accomplishments. It is not surprising that Tag Heuer has seen a spectacular rise in fortunes since tying up with Tiger Woods. Therefore, we think that the hub endorsements that tend to work and endure over the long run are those that seem to the public as being logical, genuine, and authentic. René Lacoste was the first in recent memory to emblazon a shirt with a business logo – the famous and distinctive green crocodile in 1933. But, by that time, Lacoste had already earned the nickname of "The Alligator" in the French press for his uncanny knack of not letting go of his rivals till he had completely vanquished them. Likewise, a chance remark by Marilyn Monroe in 1953 turned Chanel No. 5 perfume into an overnight sensation. She had commented to an interviewer that she wore nothing except "two drops" of the No. 5 to bed. The question was spontaneous and so was the reply. There is no evidence that there was any commercial motive or that she was paid to offer the endorsement. But, that brief incidental comment got a lot of publicity and millions of women sought to acquire a bit of the glamour and allure of the actress by adopting her favorite perfume as their own personal talisman.

The television talk show host Oprah Winfrey is a very influential hub and her on-screen views and pronouncements resonate with a large number of American women. It helps a great deal that she does not have any vested commercial motive and that she genuinely seems to look out for the interest of her audience. Consequently, when she mentions a good book she has read or a new health regimen she has tried, each becomes an instantaneous national success. In fact, Oprah's opinions carry so much weight that a number of other individuals have become famous only through being "connected" to her in one capacity or another. Thus, her personal psychologist Dr Phil McGraw became a best-selling author and the host of *his* own talk show. Bob Greene, her fitness trainer, and Art Smith, her personal chef, have achieved similar successes. That is the power of a true, modern-day hub – the Midas-like ability to raise the value of people and things, but which works only when it is granted in an honest and spontaneous manner, without a hidden agenda for recognition and profits. Marketers need to awake to these ideas to make best use of celebrity endorsements.

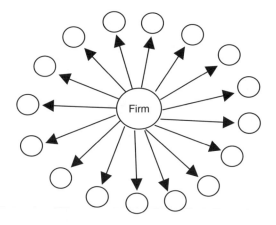

Figure 4.1 The traditional directive marketing model

So, let us look at the way that the new marketing game is shaping up in the present networked
society. Consider Figure 4.1. This is the traditional
model of marketing action – the classic push marketing paradigm. Firms have long used the "directive"
dissemination of information about their products to
end-customers in order to build their brands. The
arrows radiating outward represent the customer-
influencing activity that the firm conducts through
television and radio advertising, sales coupons, and
other forms of push marketing. As has been stated
in the previous chapters, this approach is proving to
be increasingly ineffective and is delivering marginal
returns at best.

The network model for today's marketing is shown in
Figure 4.2. Here, it is not the firm that takes center-
stage but the hub. The hub, as we have discussed,
is in essence an opinion leader, a person who com-
mands authority in a society or country (e.g., through

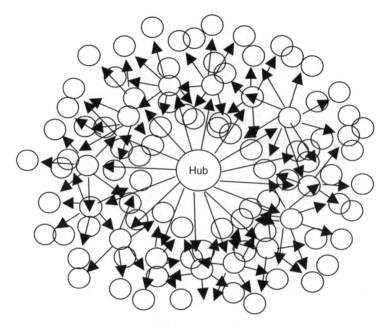

Figure 4.2 The buzz marketing model

his or her celebrity status) and who can generate the maximum number of network connections. To the extent the hub can seed and propagate a network through his own influence, while aided and assisted by word-of-mouth publicity, the firm benefits as a result. Then, the top dollars spent for this person's endorsement is money well spent. It is an important point to note that in this scheme *the firm has no overt role to play*. The logic for this follows from reverse psychology. If the firm attempts to push itself to the forefront, being seen alongside the hub, then consumer cynicism and resentment will set in quickly. The feeling among them will then be, "Why, it's the same old marketing tactics again."

Instead, the firm should attempt to stay as much as possible away from the limelight. They should allow the hub to spread the initial positive information about the product. The endorsement should seem, and in fact ideally *be*, as genuine and spontaneous as possible. Only that is capable of influencing the target audience. Then, the people – the individual nodes – of the network will take the information, try the brand, spread the word about it in their immediate circles (if the product is indeed worthwhile), and the resulting network will grow in a snowballing effect. Therefore, the role of the hub is to facilitate the network to develop and grow *on its own* through the viral interactions of people. The process will then seem natural and logical, without the intervention of a company or an external force that is calculated to arouse suspicion and cynicism. These are exactly the tactics that Red Bull used that made it into such a youth phenomenon. In the beginning, when very few people knew about Red Bull, the company actually paid bartenders to popularize cocktails with the energy drink in bars and nightclubs. It also recruited students in Europe to seed the stories about the supposed benefits and effects of consuming Red Bull, that of stamina and staying power – important for late night study and other activities in which students commonly engage. These stories spread like wildfire among young people in Europe and then around the world, no doubt distorted and made more colorful as they went from person to person, but all to Red Bull's advantage.

The following two examples also show how such a principle works in practice. Manolo Blahnik shoes gained a cult following among American women largely because of the primetime endorsement the designer received from the actress Sarah Jessica Parker in the hit HBO show *Sex and the City*. There was, in fact, an entire episode woven around Manolo Blahnik shoes. The connection worked very well because, as is widely reported, Ms Parker has a passion for shoes and she *is* a genuine fan of her Manolo's.

Pout, a niche cosmetic brand, has also followed this *same* new-age script of marketing through viral publicity. Presently, it is a rage among European and American women. The firm was started in London in 2001 by three young women, who, as is so often the case, were not happy with the existing choices in make-up. Their idea was to design a cosmetic that would convey a sense of fun and sexiness to women of all ages. From a single store (aptly called "Poutlet") in Covent Garden, the brand is now sold in over 100 stores and has close to $15 million in sales. All of this has been achieved in such a short time, and without much conventional marketing, that co-founder Emily Cohen mused to *The Sunday Times* of London, "I never thought things would take off so quickly." The reason, of course, is the connectedness of modern society and its attendant word-of-mouth dissemination. In Pout's case, it was easier and faster to ramp up the network because a number of prominent and "well-networked" women celebrities lent it their genuine and unqualified support. It was later reported that Cohen had hired the pop star Kylie Minogue's make-up artist Caroline Barnes, who also influenced her famous client to try out the new cosmetics. Word soon spread in fashion magazines and the gossip circuit that Kylie Minogue, Jennifer Lopez, Kate Hudson, Gwyneth Paltrow, and Beyoncé Knowles like Pout products and use them regularly. These stars are the present paragons of feminine beauty, and their choices in cosmetics would naturally and unquestionably command considerable influence over young women of today. So, it is not a surprise then that the brand should take off so quickly. That is the key to branding today.

Other ways to seed the network

The role of hubs is no doubt important in today's networked society, but it is not the sole means of seeding and growing a brand network. We have already discussed the idea of attracting customers by advancing the profile of a "typical customer" like the easyCustomer or the "Virgin customer". If such a customer prototype is interesting enough and is able to resonate with a sufficiently large number of people, there is a good chance that alone will succeed in piecing together a sizeable customer network. The technologies of today like the Internet, blogs, podcasting, message boards, all seem tailor-made to spread the buzz and chatter about new products. The producers of two recent hit films *The Passion of the Christ* and

The Chronicles of Narnia actively utilized Christian organizations in churches (e.g., Bible study groups) and on the Internet to seed the phenomena that both eventually became at the box-office.

In recent times there is a frequently occurring trend that a company or a creator behind a new product or a new offering merely plants the ideas and information on the Internet, or someone does it for them, and then the web-surfers spread the word-of-mouth on their own without needing any incentive or prompting. We have already referred to the Dyson vacuum cleaner and *The Da Vinci Code*, both of which benefited from the free buzz circulating on the Internet. *Arctic Monkeys*, the latest pop sensation, offers an interesting case in point. It started out as a nondescript group of four publicity-shy teenagers from High Green, Sheffield, who wanted to write and play music in their spare time. But the success that this band has had lately in the charts can only be described as mind-boggling. Their first two songs quickly became number one on pop billboards with no marketing whatsoever and without the backing of a major music studio. Their first album even went on to become the fastest selling debut album *ever* in Britain. What is perhaps even more remarkable is that all of this has been achieved by the group *with very little actual effort on their part*! It all started with a few demo CDs that they had handed out at some local performances. Someone launched a homemade website with their profiles and some free downloadable songs. This sparked the subsequent craze. As Internet buzz took over, people started trading songs to one other and their music and private lives were being constantly discussed on MySpace, the popular teen portal. All the while, the members of the group were unaware that they and their music have become so famous on the web. They have, in fact, kept a very low profile and even avoided giving interviews to the media. Nonetheless, now the *Arctic Monkeys* are being compared to *The Beatles*.

Examples also abound of more traditional firms that have achieved a similar level of market success, not necessarily by using the Internet, but by paying due attention to their customer networks and by patiently investing in a core group of buyers to develop their brands. This idea accounts for the Swiss pharmaceutical firm Novartis's rapid growth in recent times. Daniel Vasella, its CEO, made a concerted and deliberate investment in building strong relationships with physicians worldwide. Louis Vuitton in Japan also benefits from the large number of "LV Clubs" where the luxury company's affluent women patrons meet and socialize at hotels and restaurants. Consider Infosys, the Indian software powerhouse. It now has a thriving global business that is outpacing many of its larger U.S. rivals. A key factor that led to its reputation in the U.S. can be traced to the network of clients Infosys built up during the years leading up to the presumed Y2K computer bug. At the time, the laborious, low-tech, and people-intensive code modifications were considered to be too cost-ineffective to interest most major American software providers. Since Infosys performed many of these jobs either directly or as a subcontractor, this gave the firm invaluable access to a large network of Western clients, including many major multinational corporations. Today, this satisfied customer network has become its most bankable asset.

In the end, what a given firm or organization does to seed its brand and customer network must necessarily follow from its own strengths, weaknesses, and market dynamics. One issue is clear. The time for applying the usual, tired tactics of advertising and promotions is over. Instead, firms should seek to try out different, novel, and counter-intuitive approaches to attract customers and grow their networks worldwide.

5

The new marketing zeitgeist

Some people's lives are shaped very much by past events that they have experienced either positively or negatively. They often look back and think to themselves "... back in those days things were still ...", or "... everything was better then ...", but perhaps also "thank goodness those days are gone". Another group tends to live more in the future. Their whole lives are oriented toward the perception that one day, yet to come, life (or whatever) will be better. In order to make sure that they do have a better future, this group of people is willing to do without a lot of things for the present. They scrimp and save so that they can make a better tomorrow. And finally, there is a third group that does exactly the opposite. They do not save for a rainy day, but say to themselves "who knows what tomorrow will bring, I want to live for today ...". This group is investing in the present, so to speak, and relishes various things in full awareness that the future may well be uncertain. The three types of people described here are well known to psychologists. They are respectively past-oriented, future-oriented, and present-oriented. The underlying concept forming these categories is what is known as "time orientation".

There is presently an interesting marketing phenomenon that our intuition would not lead us to expect given the usual ideas. On the contrary, we would expect just the opposite. It is marketing that is always trying to emphasize how *new* a product or a service offering is. Usually, we are presented with some breakthrough, progress, innovation, etc. in one form or another, such as Procter & Gamble's "new and improved Tide detergent". As a result, marketing can be considered in general terms to be present-oriented, and in some cases even as future-oriented. There is now a trend that is contrary to this supposition, however, in that there are more and more *past-oriented* products and services in modern marketing (see Figure 5.1). And what is even more surprising is that this trend is actually catching on in many countries. There is currently a worldwide "retro" movement whereby people are seeking to reconnect with

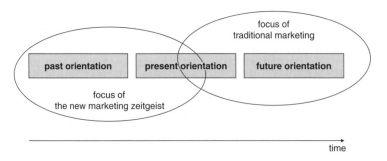

Figure 5.1   The changing orientation of time in marketing

a simpler lifestyle, one that is neither independent nor adversarial of nature, and which values the traditions and rituals of everyday life that were on the verge of getting lost. Witness the onset of the "slow food" revolution in Europe and America, widespread popularity of organic and non-GM food, and even of "log cabin" homes (which are not devoid of the most modern amenities, however) among affluent Americans. Recent years have also seen the rebirth of the opera in the West, revival of the traditional Kabuki theatre and the tea ceremony in Japan, and a renewed global interest in age-old health and fitness regimens like the Indian yoga, Chinese acupuncture, and the Japanese *shiatsu*.

It is of fundamental importance for the success of any given company to move with the times at least in terms of the products and services it offers. The German word zeitgeist (literally, spirit of the time) is a felicitous term that describes the themes and ideas that are symbolic archetypes of a certain period. Here is a time-tested and foolproof business axiom. If a commercial product or service is able to capture the zeitgeist or cater to it in some apt fashion, it stands to become a readymade success, and possibly even a cult favorite. Consider the American automobile market to find illustrations of such developing themes and trends over the last decades. Nothing symbolized the carefree and bohemian 1960s more than the VW Beetle and the Ford Mustang, which were also colossal product successes of the time. In contrast, the introspective, anti-authoritarian (viz., Watergate), fuel-strapped, stagflation-ridden years of the 1970s ushered in the era of the small, cost conscious Japanese cars like the Datsun and the Honda. The 1980s saw the growing size, confidence, and affluence of suburban families reflected in the Dodge Minivan, the prototypical auto-brand of the period. The 1990s were the time of the large, off-road vehicles and the SUV (sports utility vehicle) became the exemplar. Recent years have seen interest in more fuel-efficient cars – perhaps, the Toyota Prius is an apt example.

From the present times, if we look at the breathtaking global successes of J.K. Rowling's Harry Potter series, Dan Brown's *The Da Vinci Code*, and the Apple iPod, we may recall the German poet Goethe's thought-provoking quote about Napoleon's meteoric career: "We all feel there must be something more in it, but we do not know what." That same inexplicable quality is shared by all of these latest commercial successes, which perhaps points to an overarching period interest in certain topics, certain benefits, and certain ideas. This is why understanding the zeitgeist is so important for marketers. We may be tempted to think that zeitgeist has a great deal to do with innovations, new products, and the like. In some cases, this may even be true. The basic philosophy underlying the innovation may be related to the zeitgeist in some inalienable way. The celebrated American inventor Thomas Edison is reputed to have once said: "Ideas are *in the air*. If I had not thought of that invention, someone else would have."

But innovation alone cannot make a zeitgeist product. Zeitgeist is inherently quite separate from innovation and innovativeness. In fact, firms all over the world introduce thousands of new products each year. Most are of an incremental nature, but a few do represent the latest advances in the technology of the time, such as the latest generations of plasma televisions and digital cameras. But the appeal of a certain innovation would be multiplied manifold if it were to channel its course into meeting the needs posed by the broader societal and marketing zeitgeist, as the examples below illustrate.

P&G's turnaround – A zeitgeist story

Analysts applaud the recent upswing in the consumer goods-maker Procter & Gamble's financial fortunes as the byproduct of its new CEO A.G. Lafley's shrewd strategies. While the latter deserves due credit for changing the company's rigid mindset, what really revived P&G was its fallback, more from accident than design, on a burgeoning consumer fad and fetish – a zeitgeist related to personal and household cleanliness. For nearly 20 years, Procter & Gamble had been struggling to find a new product success. One may know that, as a company, P&G's history and roots are steeped in innovation and that many of its brands are everyday household icons. After all, it came up with Ivory – the first soap *that floated*, Pampers – the first functional disposable diaper, Crisco – the all-vegetable shortening, Pringle potato-chips – that immaculately retain their shape in its innovative tennis-ball canister. Yet, throughout the 1980s and 1990s, P&G was hard-pressed to replicate its past consumer successes with a *new* cash-cow product. Olestra, its over-hyped fat substitute, proved to be a dud.

Things began to turn around with the unexpected consumer acceptance of the Swiffer dust mop. What happened subsequently can be called a minor miracle. P&G introduced a host of new cleanliness products, from the hugely successful Crest White-strips to whiten teeth to a wide succession of Swiffer extensions. The market acceptance of all these products was boosted by the zeitgeist underlying the consumer quest for cleanliness. Consequently, the company's prospects have not looked better in a long time.

The global "slow food" movement

The marketing zeitgeist also may be viewed through the prism of the grassroots consumer movements that have taken hold in various countries. One, in particular, that seems to have slipped below the radar of the business press, but is noteworthy of our attention, is the "slow food revolution".

This movement started as a reaction against fast food and how it supposedly is resulting in the world-wide homogenization of diet. A group of European restaurateurs and consumer activists rebelled against the whole concept, which, though offering meals on the ready, has the documented consequences of obesity in children and adults, destruction of local food traditions, and the debasement of the ritual of eating. The slow food institution was founded in Bra, Italy, in 1986, shortly after the opening of the country's first McDonald's. Since then, it has grown below the glare of publicity, and the philosophy has been endorsed both by haute-cuisine restaurants and small family-owned inns. It now boasts of 83,000 members worldwide and has offices in Italy, Germany, Switzerland, the U.S., France, Japan, and Great Britain. Its stated aim is that it "opposes the standardization of taste, defends the need for consumer information, protects cultural identities tied to food and gastronomic traditions, safeguards foods and cultivation and processing techniques inherited from tradition, and defends domestic and wild animal and vegetable species." The slow food revolution has now been formalized into the nomination of around 100 towns in various countries as being officially "slow cities", that is, urban areas that restrict the use of motor vehicles, and operation of fast-food establishments and franchise enterprises on high streets.

Major aspects of the present marketing zeitgeist

We have identified three key aspects of the contemporary marketing zeitgeist. They are derived from the crying consumer need for things that are (a) simple, (b) traditional, and (c) natural.

Simple

When the last remaining VCRs were pulled off the shelves of electronics stores across the world, some newspaper critics saw an underlying social commentary. It was the demise of complexity and the rebirth of "the simple". Many cried "good riddance" to see the last of these notoriously complicated devices that had caused hair-tearing frustration and stultifying humiliation to their owners over many years. The idea that is now taking root is that things should be kept as simple as possible. Products and services must be easy to use, have readily understood features, and, importantly, facilitate or reduce the arduous chore of decision-making in their categories. It is, of course, easier said than done but brands that have especially catered to this need have fared very well recently.

The reason why such a commonsense principle should be important to uphold is that complexity in products has long been seen as a virtue and even as a consumer benefit. For almost a generation, the conventional wisdom about technological contraptions has been that "complexity pays". Manufacturers thus sought to outdo one another by loading their offerings with a veritable plethora of features and functions in a strange and self-defeating game of one-upmanship. It followed from their flawed notions that they needed to cover everything their rivals gave and do a bit more, and that "more is better" in the eyes of customers. The resulting products came with an encyclopedia-like manual and could bemuse even the hardened technology experts (more on this below). Consequently, those that have placed their faith on simplicity are beginning to reap the rewards because it exploits the present "retro" trends, besides offering an elemental consumer advantage. We should point out here, of course, that the demand for "simple" is not one that is limited to certain sections of the population (e.g., senior citizens). This is a broad-based and general phenomenon that encompasses all age groups, as the examples that follow show.

Those who know vouch that the iPod product from Apple took off in such a spectacular fashion because it is intrinsically *a very simple device*. The operations are so straightforward that one does not need to have consulted a manual to begin using it. The iPod, however, is an aberration in the crowded and complicated market of modern-day gadgets. There is a widespread belief among the technology marketers that it is becoming rather difficult to offer customers something that will genuinely pique their interest. Not because there are not enough technical inventions and functions, but quite the contrary – because there are, in fact, too many function and feature-rich gadgets. It is common knowledge that most users make use of only a fraction of the functions that are available within high-tech items. The joke about not knowing how to program a VCR could be applied today about how to navigate the complexities of a modern-day mobile phone or a digital camera. Consequently, people have become more cautious and critical when assessing the merits of the latest gadget, and perhaps justifiably so. Most are unable to cope with the available items. There are usually many functions that can accomplish things in new, interesting, and innovative ways, but very few people really know how to make use of them. To that extent, technology represents a great opportunity lost in terms of value and cost.

The Blackberry pocket organizer, the Dyson vacuum cleaner, and the ultra-slim Motorola Razr mobile phone testify to the significant potential to earn high margins from a well-designed, easy-to-use, and truly superior product. These products could be said to have followed in the footsteps of the iconic European brands like Bang and Olufsen and the Vertu phone, which have long established how such a product concept can win a devoted following. The key lies in design, of course – one that is clever, eye-catching, and memorable. In a previous chapter, we have already mentioned how the design or *soft quality* of products has now become a critical differentiating advantage, given that functional quality has become easily attainable in most categories.

Consider as well the following instances that capture the idea of "simplicity marketing".

■ The ever-growing popularity of IKEA stores and their furniture is testament to the power of "simple". In fact, IKEA store openings have caused well-publicized stampedes in countries around the world. The appeal of this Swedish retailer rests in its simple, minimalist furniture at prices that are well within the middle-class family's budget. (Of course, for a non-do-it-yourselfer assembling the furniture at home is anything but simple!)

- Citigroup, the world's largest bank, has recently unveiled a new credit card called *Simplicity* which promises to make everything simple, including the ready availability of a customer service operator.

- Adidas markets its soccer shoes using the tagline "Simplicity is bliss".

- Skagen watches from Denmark have caught on because of their simple and slim design without any ostentatious extras.

- A book called *Simplify Your Life* written by Elaine St. James became a national bestseller in the U.S. It offered such tips and social wisdom as: "Move to a smaller house", "Get out of debt", and "Always split a restaurant meal".

- A lot of young people like Puma, New Balance, and Asics shoes, which are relatively simple and plain-looking, because they have an understated marketing approach compared with their more glitzy rivals, Nike and Adidas-Reebok.

- There is a growing tendency to market various combination or all-in-one types of products in various categories, such as an all-in-one cold remedy (i.e., which addresses all cold and flu symptoms), dish-washing liquid and hand lotion, Gillette shavers with integrated after-shave lotion, printer-copier-scanner, and so on.

Traditional

This is again a pervasive trend all over the world, whereby ideas for products and their designs that were popular many decades ago are making a successful comeback. Luxury items that till recently may have seemed gaudy, passé, and out-of-vogue, like fancy canes, cigarette cases and holders, music boxes, jewelry cases, and decorative clothes boxes, are gaining favor once more among the moneyed classes. *Bunny London*, a British apparel boutique, has revived the lacy and frilly children's dress designs from a bygone age much as parents would choose in the Victorian era. This brand and its items have received public support from the celebrity artiste Madonna, who reportedly buys them for her daughter Lourdes. Often, the reasons why "old is gold" at the present time have less to do with what had made them popular before, but are derived instead from the expediencies of contemporary life. People these days are looking for things that are distinctive and classy – they feel that the modern age has undermined the craftsmanship of industry and standardized everything by producing them from factories and conveyor belts. Hence, the renewed interest in well-aged cognac, fine cigars, mechanized watches, bespoke Savile Row suits, and

custom-made Berluti shoes. In America the Nick-
elodeon television channel, which shows reruns of
the popular shows from the 1950s and 1960s, has
garnered a large fan-base. It attracts mostly middle-
aged viewers, who perhaps seek to reconnect with
their younger years. But, interestingly, many watch
them with their children to expose them to a simpler and far more innocent time, in contrast to
the sex-and-violence-ridden fare that is commonly
on view.

Some additional examples:

- In the auto industry, models and designs are being
  relaunched that were once popular, but had disappeared from view for many years. The Chrysler
  PT Cruiser, Volkswagen Beetle, Ford Mustang,
  and the BMW Mini are notable instances. The
  Porsche motor company has played up to the traditional appeal by preserving the look and feel of
  the 911 make for more than 40 years, which is
  considered rather unusual in the car industry.

- Nivea, the iconic German skin-care brand, has
  found renewed favor among the world's youth.
  The brand, which was founded in 1911, is still
  going strong in Europe, Asia, and America.

- In India, the hookah, a homegrown pipe for
  smoking tobacco, is making a colorful return
  among the rich and sophisticated set. Once
  derided as being the habit of the lower classes,
  hookah smoking is the new vogue, and a number

of chic bars have been launched in the major Indian cities for that purpose.

- More and more young women in the West are choosing to wear pearl jewelry, which was popular with their grandmothers in the 1940s and 1950s but then fell out of favor. Pearls are the fashion now, more than the gold and silver of recent years.

- Some years ago, a book about consumer nostalgia was published in the German-speaking countries of Europe. Entitled *Wickie, Slime und Paiper*, it listed a variety of everyday products that were popular in the German market about 30 years earlier, but which then became obsolete and defunct. The book was a huge success, and a second volume was published soon afterward. There was even a television show based on the same nostalgia concept. Much more interesting, however, was the public pressure that was subsequently laid on the company that had sold "Paiper ice-cream" decades ago. Although, production of the ice-cream had long since stopped, following the success of the book and because of the clamor and outcry from its readers, it had to be resumed and offered again, and the product sold out very quickly.

- In the new free-market countries of Eastern Europe, including the former East Germany, Russia, Bulgaria, Romania, and the Czech Republic, an interesting brand phenomenon took place recently. Products such as cars, televisions, and refrigerators that were once preferred during the Communist years made a winning return, usually infused with Western technology and quality standards. The trend became pervasive enough that it was given a name: *ostalgie* (or nostalgia for the East).

Natural

The third aspect of today's marketing zeitgeist is the increasingly visible and surprising popular urge to reconnect with nature and to adopt a lifestyle that is less reliant on technology and machines, but more in harmony with the human and natural world. In fact, a pervasive and growing trend among the educated classes of Western Europe and America is to avoid food containing GM ingredients, derisively referred to as Frankenfoods. There are certain widespread beliefs that these modern techniques have contaminated the food chain by needlessly interfering with nature, and that the resulting offerings may even be bad for health. Accordingly, a large number of consumers have embraced stores and labels that sell organic produce even though the prices they pay there are considerably higher than at supermarket chains. In the U.S., Whole Foods Market and Trader Joe's (owned by the German Aldi chain), both of which advance this organic and small farm-grown philosophy, have been gaining a mass following. When the first Whole Foods store opened in downtown Manhattan recently, checkout lines were crowded as had not been seen previously. Similarly, weekend farmer's markets in small towns all across America have never been busier.

In Austria, an organic private label called *Ja! Natür-lich* (i.e., Yes! Naturally) offers a widely acclaimed "holiday on the farm" program for families with children to meet the organic farmers and producers in their own setting. The firm asserts, with justi-fiable logic, that this program offers city kids the chance that they normally would not have, to see the open country and to know how milk and eggs are produced. But this interest really extends beyond children. One of the better aspects of organic farm-ing is the understanding that consumers should be curious to know from where the food on their plates has actually originated. In a globalized economy such as ours, that supply chain is largely obfuscated, hence some stores have taken it upon themselves to identify the sources of the fruit, vegetables, meats, and fish – even down to the name of the actual farmer, butcher, and trader. Interestingly, this has led to a situation where shoppers are happiest with a product that comes from their own region, and even where they perhaps know the producer personally.

Some more instances are as follows:

■ Prince Charles, heir to the British throne, was one of the earliest proponents of the bene-fits of organic farming and the possible ills of factory-oriented mass production of food. While suffering ridicule in the past by the popular media, he seems to have been finally vindicated. Not only are his views becoming widely accepted, the *Duchy Originals* brand of organic foodstuffs produced from his Cornish estate under strict natural conditions has fared very well in recent years.

■ More and more people from the educated classes of the West are embracing an all-vegetarian diet for health, dietary, or humanitarian reasons.

■ There is now a well-established global trend of consuming bottled mineral water as an accompaniment to meals instead of carbonated soft drinks, juices, and even wines. Clean and pure spring water is fast becoming a precious, marketable resource.

■ A small but influential group of celebrities have made "oxygen bars", which supposedly revitalize and energize the body, cool and stylish in cities like New York, London, and Tokyo.

■ There is now an increasing use of aromatherapy as a therapeutic technique.

■ Finally, a large number of products have made nature and natural ingredients the central aspect of their marketing and branding strategies, for example, Burt's Beeswax products in the U.S., Cold-Eaze lozenges, Natural Instincts hair-color for women, Herbal Essence shampoos, Aveda cosmetics, and JS Natural Hemp clothing.

What are the macro-societal reasons for these trends? Why are people buying simple, traditional, and natural products more than before?

1. *Complexity of the choice process*: For an increasing number of people, going to a mall, store, or supermarket can be an unwelcome experience. Many complain that shopping actually causes them stress. The principal reason for this is the vast number of shopping choices on offer, which makes people dread about making the wrong decision. The problem is aggravated when one has to make a high-ticket purchase, since then the financial consequences of making a mistake loom very large indeed. In the past, if a customer had a problem with a product he bought or if he wanted information regarding a certain feature, he could call the customer help desk and have his problem resolved quickly by an agent. Nowadays, that same customer has to talk to an automated phone-line, choose numbers from a set menu, punch the buttons incessantly, and, in the end, if he is lucky, he might be allowed to talk to a real person. So, the penalty of making a mispurchase has increased substantially.

   In the past, brands were good tools for many customers to gain some orientation and insight within the complex market setting. If someone wanted to buy a new camera, he often did not know the specific features, but he knew he was going to buy a Canon or a Yashica. But, lately the branded companies have introduced such a profusion of line extensions, with their alphabet soup names, that the customer is left totally confused (see discussion in Chapter 2). Some years ago, Mercedes stood solely for luxury and exclusivity, and, accordingly, its cars sold at a very high price. Now, Mercedes has extended its product range – below the S-Class, E-Class, now there are also smaller and cheaper cars available in the A-, B-, and C-Classes. So, the more a company extends the brand, the less clear is the picture that it conveys to its customers. Accordingly, it gets that much harder for the poor customer to find his bearings in a complex market. Not unexpectedly, anything that tends to simplify the situation finds grateful acceptance by the public.

2. *Complexity of the product or service itself*: Moreover, even if someone decides to buy a particular product and finds one suited for his purpose, he is then faced with an onerous "homework", to make sense of the scores of functions that the item, particularly if it is high-tech, is likely to have. Reading a modern-day technology manual has become the equivalent of having one's teeth being extracted. One may say that marketing is the culprit here, since it is a fundamental role of marketing to offer choices, options, and variety, but more choices do end up causing buying stress. So, a little bit of reverse psychology and counter-intuitive (from the firm's viewpoint) tactics are in order. Incidentally, a lot

of services, like banks, brokerage, insurance, and hospitals, are becoming more complex as well. At an ATM in Europe, people can withdraw cash, load money onto their cards, buy credit for their phones, and so on. Of course, most people like the services very much, but quite a few tend to suffer stress navigating through the menu options when there are 10 other people waiting in line behind them. In a situation like this, it is hardly surprising that products and services that are easy to understand and operate should enjoy market success.

3. *Changing values and beliefs*: People in Western societies have become increasingly conscious of their life-styles, food intake, and exercise regimens. They are well abreast of the recent medical advances, up-and-coming drugs, and media debates about the pros and cons of genetic modification of food. Most of them are able to make up their own minds on which side they stand. Generally speaking, European consumers tend to be more demanding than their American and Asian counterparts about the integrity of food, although the latter are catching up as well.

There is besides a general perception that life today has become too complex, that technology advances are too hard to keep up with, and that businesses often profit from people's ignorance about these matters. Accordingly, for many there is a deep yearning and nostalgia for the past, when everything seemed better, easier, slower,

and cleaner (i.e., less-polluted). One could argue
that frequently the reason for this is simply happy
memories from one's younger days. In psychology, this phenomenon is known as positive past-
orientation. Many people make a link in their
minds between certain pleasant experiences in
their past (say, involving family members and
pets) to certain commercial products. Some grew
up hearing stories of things they never used but
which were part of their parents' and grandparents' lives. This perhaps partly accounts for
the revival of and reconnection to products and
brands from a far previous generation.

4. *Aging of Western societies*: Although we should
emphasize that the desire for simple products is
evident across all age groups, it is fast becoming
the norm among the aged and the elderly. Note
that the average age in Western societies is rising
all the time. In many European countries and in
the U.S., more than half of the population will
be over 50 years old in 20 years' time. While
the willingness to deal with new and complicated
items varies from one person to the next, unfor-
tunately, certain abilities do diminish with age.
There comes a time when the means of absorbing
certain things in every detail, as is required for
the highly complicated menus in mobile phones,
become limited or impaired. In Japan, where the
population is aging very rapidly, mobile operat-
ors have launched a device called TuKa that is
very simple indeed. Its sole feature is the phone –
the ability to make and receive mobile calls – and

no additional functions like messaging, camera, web access, clock, alarm, and so on. It also has bigger buttons than the usual cell phone, much louder sound volume, and larger battery capacity, which necessitates less frequent recharges. All of this seems ideally suited for the older customer. Interestingly, however, TuKa sales have taken off slowly since there is a perception among some potential customers that its use would invite ridicule and a loss of "face" – an unthinkable prospect in a traditional Oriental society.

5. *Sinking credibility of large firms*: Finally, the factor accounting for at least some of the aspects of the present zeitgeist could be the highly publicized, recent developments in the corporate arena that have shown large multinational companies in a poor light. Various scandals, where the company management lined their own pockets at the expense of shareholders, when compromises were made threatening food and drug safety, where child labor was used, etc., have contributed to a marked drop in the overall credibility of firms. Indeed, tantalizing news accounts of the story and scandals underlying the rise and fall of Enron – tales of sleaze and greed – have been followed with avidity by the general public. Enron has now become the symbol of all that is wrong in the business world. And, quite unfairly, the public tends to paint large companies by the same wide brush. As a result, it is all the more difficult nowadays for firms to market their products with the boldness and bravado as they used to before.

The present time thus calls for an understated tone in the marketing and advertising.

Zeitgeist and reverse psychology marketing

It goes without saying that marketing has in some way got to target the needs, desires, and aspirations of the target consumer. In the final analysis, a firm depends on this ability to sell its products and services. Consequently, the idea of bringing the zeitgeist into consideration for better marketing is not exactly new or surprising. What is surprising, however, is the fact that, under closer scrutiny, the current zeitgeist contains several aspects that would not have been expected in this form. One would more likely have expected the reverse for nearly all of these aspects.

The desire for simpler products and services would be easy to understand if we were to look at all the complicated technical products on the market today. Still, the natural inclination for manufacturers remains to do exactly the opposite. At every new product launch or relaunch, it is very common to see that firms have added new functions and features to give birth to a highly sophisticated yet highly complex contraption, and their sales managers gloat over them as a proud parent would at a nursery. No one bothers to question whether the added functions deliver significant incremental value, and whether the customer should need them at all. The idea of *subtracting* features to aid simplicity and usability does not seem to enter the picture. Or, something that could be smarter, the notion of designing products in such a fashion that the functions are easily understood and operated is yet to resonate with manufacturers in a meaningful way. Yet, if we consider the strategies of companies in recent times, we see several instances of firms that have achieved success by working from the reverse mentality. Nokia has managed to beat cheaper Chinese rivals in their own backyard by adopting such an idea. The firm has been very successful selling smart-looking phones *that are also very easy to use* to the semi-literate peasants in the farthest reaches of China. Nokia is now attempting to do the same in India. Dyson vacuum cleaners have overtaken the redoubtable Hoover by working from a very similar notion. Dysons are simply designed, *without* a lot of "attachments" and even look somewhat old-fashioned. But they do *one* thing exceptionally well, which is to remove dust – the intended function (and desired utility) of a vacuum cleaner. We should not find it surprising then how quickly this product has gained acceptance among customers all over the world, even achieving a cult-like following.

As for the growing number of "retro" products that hark back to bygone times, another reverse mindset is at play here as well. Marketing, since its inception, has been largely present- or future-oriented. The emphasis has always seemed to be on progress, innovation, development, and breakthrough in one shape or another. Advertisements have always seemed to cry out loud "Look how things are better than before" or "The future will be better with these products". That there could be an *innate* virtue to things that have a long history and tradition was less well understood or appreciated. This was particularly true of Americans, understandably, perhaps, because of their New World mindset, than Asians or Europeans. Consequently, the line "*Since* such-and-such date" ("*Depuis* . . .", as in French, "*Seit* . . ." as in German, etc.) hardly ever appears on American labels, even for products with century-old traditions, like Kodak and Gillette.

But now that orientation appears to be changing. The consumers' nostalgic yearning for things of the past is finally finding an outlet. It has been reported that there is an increasing trend among affluent American city-dwellers to get a log cabin home in the country – and, for some it is even their only home. The romantic appeal is well understood, recalling a far more innocent and pristine time when people lived in communion with nature. There is also an added association perhaps with Abraham Lincoln – the most favorite U.S. president of all time – and stories of his idyllic childhood. It should be pointed out, however, that these so-called "log cabins" are now equipped with the latest in technology and gadgetry so that their occupants do not have to suffer the same privations of their nineteenth-century ancestors.

The discussion relating to natural products has been going on quite some time. But, such notions as slow food, vegetarianism, organic produce, and nature therapy were limited before to a very small minority of urbanites who were typically very well educated and somewhat left-leaning. Indeed, those who espoused such views, royalty included, were seen as being somewhat eccentric and ridiculed in the popular press for being anti-modernist Luddites (or cult-worshipping hippies). It is therefore interesting to observe how such seemingly "extreme" viewpoints have become more acceptable having been embraced by the global mainstream. A second point is that while in the past people sometimes said that they considered natural products to be important for their health and the ecology, they often did not buy them. Price was the main hurdle. However, that behavior seems to be changing. Consumers not only believe that natural products make more sense, but they are actually purchasing them in large quantities as well. In this connection, we should mention that the term "natural" is intended here in the broadest sense of the word. Often, the customer's main aim is to be able to consume *authentic* products (more on this in Chapter 7). These are the things that are made while forsaking any compromise with the expediencies of a mass-marketing and profit-seeking corporation and while respecting the ecological interplay of man and nature. In the long run, it is that credibility that counts for the consumer of today.

6

The era of anti-marketing

A strange and curious phenomenon is unfolding around us without the knowledge of most of us, but with profound significance for the way we understand and do business. A small but influential group of firms are doing things and implementing ideas that are daring to defy the norms and conventions which traditional marketing theory considers as articles of faith. They seem to flout every known precept, every bedrock axiom of the traditional theory, which a businessperson knows by rote – that a firm should publicize its offerings, reach out to customers, cater to their needs, and maintain close relationships with them. Instead, these new ventures actively shun publicity, make it harder for people to find their establishments, then unilaterally dictate what they can have, and offer very little choice or flexibility overall. Yet, they manage to sell a lot of their products at exceptionally high margins. How do they do it? Viewed from these developments, one may think that a new contrarian age is dawning. It seems to favor a new breed of entrepreneurs and business models that are grounded in unmistakably reverse psychology concepts.

It is important to understand that anti-marketing is not a development against business or against globalization. It is a new way of selling that is perhaps more honest and less pretentious (or spin-prone), arising as a logical outgrowth from the present business climate and consumer ethos. Its votaries do not shun pecuniary benefits or modern business methods, but many are socially conscious and appreciate the symbiotic relationship that exists between business and society. Some view their products much like works of art and understand that making them seem unattainable increases their selling potential. The best proponents of anti-marketing are those that appear genuine because of the reputation they have earned either for their exacting standards or for their quirky personalities and untrammeled lifestyles. Consequently, their novel, counter-intuitive, and unscripted selling approaches have the capacity to interest the buyer. From that perspective, anti-marketing is a very clever instance of pull marketing.

Take the case of Nigo, an eccentric, soft-spoken, and reclusive former Japanese DJ, who came up with a brand called A Bathing Ape (BAPE for short). BAPE started with T-shirts, and then metamorphosed into a lifestyle company selling baggy jeans, sneakers, music, and food. Each item of clothing sports a small icon, a trademark gorilla-head – that's it. But, BAPE is now a global cult brand that has a growing and ardent fan following, including several high-profile celebrities, and all of this has been achieved without a single promotional ad. In fact, Nigo goes to extreme lengths to shun advertising and publicity and actively discourages celebrities from being photographed in his label. He has been quoted as saying, "I really do not want a lot of people wearing my clothes." Part of the mystique lies in how difficult it is to find a store and purchase the items. Nigo does not advertise the location, and storefronts are intentionally unmarked with a very fine etching of the word 'Nowhere' above the front entrance. Customers are made to wait in line to get into the store. Then they are allowed to buy only one item and that too in their own sizes. Nigo's first and only store in the U.S. opened in New York's Soho district attracting a crowd through only word-of-mouth publicity.

The above notions of exclusivity and unattainability are also behind the new crop of shops, restaurants, and nightclubs that are opening each year in every metropolis. They renounce overt signage and make it difficult for people who are not in the know to find them. The idea is if you do not know what it is and where it is, you have no business being there. These businesses thrive from the buzz and chatter created by their regular customers. Such shops are common in Tokyo's Harajuku district, the source of many *avant-garde* global youth trends. Similar motifs are to be seen in Paris, London, and New York. *Confidential*, a trendy new restaurant that opened at San Diego in 2005, also lives up to its name. It is located in an unmarked building, has bouncers at the entrance, and the food and service are good enough to keep up the appeal and mystique. Another popular anti-marketing tactic is to place a trendy nightclub or bistro in a run-down, decrepit, and even crime-prone urban neighborhood. The aim perhaps is to invoke a "contrast effect" and also to insert an element of danger and risk. In Miami there is a high-end nightclub called *Club Space* that looks just like a dilapidated warehouse from the outside and is located in a dubious part of the city. Yet, this club is very popular with the city's celebrities and its youth, especially at late hours when the other bars and clubs close down. Some of these establishments lay down strict dress rules and other restrictions about what clients can or cannot have to reinforce the view that it is *they* who have been graced by their admittance. In this context, the *omakase* (or "chef's choice") concept arising from the Japanese culinary tradition has become exceptionally popular. Here, customers have no decision-making power once they have reserved a table and sat down to eat. They have to eat whatever the chef has selected to cook that day.

How anti-marketing creates the pull dynamic

One of the essential elements of traditional marketing is the customer orientation. This means that the customers' wants and desires are central to the company's focus and all of its marketing activities like new product development, communication, distribution, etc. are geared around them. While that seems logical in theory, in practice it has been overdone to such an extent that either the buyers have lost interest or there are diminishing marginal returns from catering to a fickle clientèle. Customers today complain of *too much* choice and too much sales pressure from direct marketing, pop-up ads, and noisy infomercials on TV and radio. Therefore, businesses that reduce choice or apply reverse-psychology to make their product seem alluring are better able to capture the buyer's attention and interest.

Consider the tactics of Philadelphia jeweler Steven Singer. He has launched a very successful anti-marketing campaign and created plenty of buzz by building from the premise that men hate the store because women love the jewelry that it sells. When driving down the I-95 highway in the eastern U.S., people are likely to see his billboards in black displaying the words: "I HATE STEVEN SINGER!" Many are intrigued by the "hate" message against the firm, enough to go to the website just to find out what the slogan is all about. Not surprisingly, the jeweler has seen a boost in traffic and sales since the campaign was started.

It is perhaps easy to disparage and dismiss these developments as passing fads, but in our view they represent a real change in business. What these anti-marketers are working from is the deep-seated consumer resentment against the prevalent norms and practices of traditional marketing. This dynamic can take several forms. Many people are simply tired of all the spin and the pretense that is commonly on view in ads and slogans. When they see a well-known movie star or athlete pushing a product, they know that the person has been generously paid to do so. Hence, the endorsement is taken with more than a pinch of salt. Vitamin Water, a new beverage, takes a refreshingly different branding approach. It competes with top-selling sports drinks like Pepsi's Gatorade and Coke's Powerade. The brand comes in different flavors, each of which is unique in content and is targeted to a specific mental or physical aspect such as focus, endurance, regeneration, and so on. Its endurance label says, "Professional athletes have not endorsed this product . . . excessive use will not lead you to be like Mike, Magic or even athletes named Ned. We rebut any offers by professional sports leagues to become the official water of anything. Although this is a great alternative to sports drinks, we do not believe in succumbing to commercialism. Unless, of course, there's a lot of cash. Then we'll talk." The last two sentences are presumably meant to be a joke and as a mild dig at their larger and better-known competitors.

By the same token, models with ethereal good looks wearing expensive clothes and hawking fancy gadgets can faze after a while. They and their lifestyles may appear unreachable and otherworldly to those simpler souls with humdrum jobs and bills to pay. This in turn creates cynicism and boredom with marketing messages. The corporate giants seem to have taken note. Unilever's recent *Dove Campaign for Real Beauty* is essentially an anti-marketing campaign that features very real people with all of their imperfections but who want to look beautiful. This campaign runs mostly print ads in women's magazines that show everyday women, young and old, with freckles, wrinkles, or buxom figures, who ask society to redefine the values of beauty.

The sort of anti-marketing that appeals to the affluent has to be perforce of a different kind. They, above all, crave privacy and exclusivity, and abhor the loud attention to places and things that are then destined to be the staples of the masses. Hordes of tourists started to overrun Provence in France and Tuscany in Italy after two popular travelogues detailing their respective charms became popular bestsellers. Consequently, recent years have seen the rise of secret, hideaway destinations, like the superexclusive Aman resorts, which cater to the global few and that operate behind the scenes away from the tourist trails. These resorts balk at publicity and over-exposure, and even reserve the right to screen their guests. The same principles account for the popularity of the anonymous restaurants and nightclubs. A new species of "travel consultants" have also arrived in every major city with decidedly anti-marketing credentials. For a fee, they provide select clients with something very valuable: access to the world's best and finest. Breathtaking beaches, private art galleries, posh apartments, hard-to-get concert tickets, special seating at restaurants, etc. – all that are distant from the well-trodden paths.

"Less" as a reverse psychology strategy

Offering less is one of the key generic ideas of anti-marketing. This tactic is the absolute opposite of the traditional strategy whereby companies usually try to improve the value for their customers by providing *more* products, *more* features, *more* services, *more* stores, and so on. The "less" strategy has different aspects, such as: (1) less information; (2) less service; (3) less choice; (4) less segmentation; and (5) less availability. The reason why "less" works in these instances is that it invokes a perception of scarcity, that things are limited or in short supply, which usually connotes desirability in the minds of buyers. For people who are far too used to seeing more, "less" obviously signifies that the items being sold must be worth having. Incidentally, the same factor accounts for the effectiveness and success of the frequently seen retailer tactic of "Limit (a certain quantity) per customer."

1. *Less information*: In every marketing textbook one reads that it is essential to educate the consumer and to publicize and "promote" a new product or service. This should mean supplying the appropriate product-related information to the public so that they can make good informed decisions. But this marketing axiom has been misconstrued and misapplied by most businesses in such a way that they have weighed consumers down by an oppressive, and usually gratuitous,

information overload. Firms now seek to outdo one another by making ever louder and more extravagant claims, which, though intended to get attention, may actually dispel it being lost in a marketing cacophony. In fact, a contemporary truism holds that an average person is exposed to more information today than a man in the Middle Ages learned in his entire lifetime! So, a message that is understated and playful (like the one on the Vitamin Water label) does not cause stress or pressure on the buyer, and is therefore more effective.

There is yet another reason why this strategy works. Less information creates a quizzical air of anticipation and mystery that is a clever pull-marketing ploy, by itself. Harry Potter's author J.K. Rowling and her publisher Bloomsbury have been known to keep the fans in suspense about the plot of a new title prior to its release. Such is the tight control of information about upcoming stories that it creates intense worldwide speculation, rumor, and gossip, all of which is enough to pull readers to the midnight launch of the books. Some firms also understand that the problem for a new restaurant, store, or resort is not too little publicity but very often *too many* people know about it. Hence, they seek to limit information to create expectation and interest. But it should be remembered that less information does not imply suppressing product flaws or potential drawbacks that a customer ought to know. Nor should it be seen as an attempt to place the customer at a deliberate information disadvantage to instill ignorance and fear in order to foist an unworthy item.

The other problem is that with too much information or publicity the "wrong" people begin to patronize the business, as what happened to the Burberry label. Then, the desired customers could perceive that they do not identify with the brand anymore, leave it altogether, and choose another. This phenomenon follows from the close relationship that exists between the brand and its customer network, which was discussed in Chapter 4.

2. *Less service*: Anti-marketing could also work by taking away certain service prerogatives that customers had hitherto considered as the norm. It is presently happening in the banking, brokerage, retail, and airline industries, though not always with sound business logic and wisdom. In the cases of banking and brokerage, people have actually welcomed the chance to do a number of activities on their own. Technology, especially the Internet, has become a useful tool to perform those tasks that a customer service person had to help with before. The hard discounters also have managed to pull this strategy off successfully in Europe and North America. Take Sam's Club and Food Basics in the U.S., Tesco and Asda in the U.K., and Aldi and Lidl in many European countries. Their main competitive advantage is that they offer products at lower prices than

the other stores. But they offer next-to-nothing by way of customer service. At most of these places one has to bag one's purchases and some even expect shoppers to bring their own bags. All of these companies make a clear statement that their prices are unbeatably low, and that promise is typically kept. So, this has brought them customer satisfaction (in a perverse way) as well as plenty of credibility.

The hard discounters have a cost structure that is quite different from those of other store-types. They have very basic facilities, less selection, less availability of national brands, more emphasis on store labels and generics, and so on. Their business philosophy is relatively simple and it is usually communicated well to customers. Although they do not offer much in terms of service, it is acceptable since they have not promised it and their customers do not therefore expect it. But, the advisability of stripping service below the expected threshold (as has happened in the airline industry) is questionable since it leaves room, the aforementioned sweet spot, for a rival to enter and exploit.

3. *Less choice*: There is a growing trend among major consumer goods companies like P&G and Unilever to reduce choice in many consumption categories, from selling *fewer* brands. This should also be seen as anti-marketing because it is contrary to the free-market ethic of more consumer choice. In effect, during the last few

years, firms have been reducing the number of brands they used to have in their portfolios. Their goal now is that each of their brands should be a category leader *à la* Jack Welch's maxim at GE. From the buyer's perspective, this development is not altogether unwelcome since fewer brands mean reduced choice complexity and less head-scratching in the shopping aisles.

Paradoxically, there is some evidence that reduced choice makes people more interested in shopping and also tends to make them more brand-loyal. Shoppers are more likely to shirk making decisions in categories where there are too many alternatives. Also, when there is more choice, they are more tempted to try out different brands on different occasions – resulting in what is mischievously called *polygamous shopping*, which is bad for the bigger brands. Hence, businesses are better off having a narrower line of brands than they did in the past.

It is also a well-known fact that many firms engaged in wide-scale product proliferation since the mid-1970s, and the results have been self-defeating and ruinous: higher administration and production costs, more buyer confusion, and reduced brand loyalty. So, it may well be time to cut back on superfluous brands. Recall, in this context, the "ostalgie" phenomenon, whereby erstwhile East Germans still yearn for items from their simpler, less consumerist days. Marketing experts generally assumed that after the walls came down, people in the former Eastern Bloc would be happier with the shopping choices available in the West and they would gladly renounce the decrepit makes of the Communist era. The fact that Trabant and Lada cars, Vita cola, and Stinol refrigerators are still holding their own against far more glitzy and sophisticated Western and Japanese competitors attests to the captivating appeal of reduced choice and simplicity.

4. *Less segmentation*: On a related theme, one of the basic marketing ideas is to build segments of potential customers and to target them with different products or services based on their specific needs and wants. Recent years have seen an anti-marketing practice, which is to abandon that well-established principle, and to offer just *one product* for all customers. That is the idea behind the new crop of all-in-one, "segment-buster" products like the Colgate Total, and new combination medicines for cold symptoms or stomach ailments. The appeal for such items among consumers is not very hard to grasp. People have become just fed up with the arbitrary and mind-numbing choices in every consumer category that have existed for far too long. There used to be (and still are) toothpastes for a particular *narrow* benefit: *either* cavity prevention or tartar-control or tooth whitening or gum strengthening, etc. Presumably, all of these variants arose to reap the supposed rewards of what is commonly called "benefit-based marketing segmentation". But the obvious consumer response

is: "Why not have everything?" It took some
time for Colgate-Palmolive to understand this
need and it became the motivation for the "anti-
segment" Colgate Total brand. Total made a very
successful market entry and propelled Colgate to
first place in the toothpaste market in the U.S.
In so doing, it displaced P&G's Crest brand to
a distant second from which the company hasn't
recovered notwithstanding its own Crest Complete brand, which incidentally draws from the
same anti-segment principle.

5. *Less availability*: It seems paradoxical that in a
   world where it is expected that all things should
   be available all of the time, there are some companies that say they will offer some products
   only for a short time. And their customers do
   not seem to mind at all. In fact, they like the
   change when explained the rationale. The Austrian
   store label *Ja! Natürlich* (literally, Yes! Naturally) sells organic produce *only* in their time-
   appropriate seasons. Buyers were made aware
   that to offer fruits and vegetables throughout the
   year would entail recourse to artificial processing
   and ripening means, which the brand strictly
   renounces. So by engaging in such a restrict-
   ive anti-marketing ploy the brand has won kudos
   and become more credible as a result! The German discounter Aldi mails a flyer every week
   to German households informing them that they
   will sell a limited product selection the following week, say TV sets, PCs, refrigerators, clothes,
   bicycles, etc. until they are sold out. Shoppers

know that they stand to reap attractive discounts only if they can avail of the opportunity. So, they come in droves. Likewise, the Tchibo/Eduscho chain of coffee shops in Europe sells a *limited* assortment of relatively expensive items (ranging from digital cameras to jewelry), and the collection changes from one week to the next. All of this is based on the store's catchy slogan "Every week a new experience".

What makes anti-marketing and reverse psychology tactics work

Customer need satisfaction is a bedrock concept in marketing. As the maxim goes, "Find wants and fill them." The corresponding anti-marketing idea is to pay less heed to what the *average customer* wants, but to do what the company thinks is right for *its own self* or for certain select customers. The "Steirereck", a famous gourmet restaurant in Vienna, offers an interesting example. A couple of years ago, the owner opened a sister restaurant in an old, traditional house situated in the Austrian Alps in the province of Styria, where Steirereck's celebrated founder Heinz Reitbauer was born. The goal for the new restaurant was mainly to attract weekend tourists. So, it only opens between Thursday and Sunday. What is more interesting is the *coup de grâce* delivered every Sunday afternoon (during the closing time) in the form of a special "dinner of the rests". Its sole purpose is to sell the leftover food from the kitchen albeit at a cut-rate price. So, at that time the guests basically have no choice but to be content with whatever food is left in the kitchen. Yet, paradoxically the restaurant is usually very busy on Sunday afternoons.

The cult-like appeal of the Italian-made Diesel jeans among the world's youth rests on the perception that it is unlike any other marketing brand. In fact, Diesel is said to be the "anti-cool" brand. Its marketing is indeed unconventional, though not gratuitously pro-vocative like Benetton, but certainly going against prevailing norms and challenging the societal stasis. This philosophy is conveyed in a somewhat ideo-logical and self-undermining way. The message is usually of the contrarian kind that Diesel will *not* make someone look more smart or attractive or help him get more friends. But, it tends to draw in large numbers those young people who profess to be cyn-ical about the exaggerated advertising claims of the other apparel marketers. To them Diesel champions a newfound spirit of truth and social justice much like Levi's epitomized freedom and rebellion to their parents and grandparents. One recent Diesel ad, for instance, shows a group of hogs seated around a table, feasting on a roasted hog. The waitress looks on, clad in a pair of Diesel jeans. It is Diesel's usual, quirky way of mocking the culture of consumption and excess. Predictably, the brand now has a devoted following in the global youth market.

Why do reverse psychology tactics work in practice? What is the underlying theory, principle, or axiom that interests people and captures their loyalty and commitment? One can advance a number of reasons to explain the effects that these techniques have on the buying public. As a general rule, anti-marketing goes against the grain of traditional marketing and suggests different ideas to each consumer. The firm is made to appear less interested in sales and profits, but more focused on advancing its own craft or a related ideology. There is no element of the usual over-catering or pandering to meet customer whims. The buyer is given a clear choice: to accept the product as is or to go somewhere else. (Of course, to execute this strategy well that product must be worth having to begin with.) This message is starkly different from the other marketers and evokes a feeling of respect and admiration among many people. There is also some measure of mystery and suspense since the seller then seems unpredictable and not following the beaten path.

The appeal of reverse psychology can be further explained from a prevailing theory of customer satisfaction. This theory suggests that a customer's satisfaction or dissatisfaction is an outcome of a comparison process. For every transaction, people compare what they received with what they had expected from the firm or the product prior to its purchase. If the brand meets or exceeds what customers had expected in the first place, then they are usually satisfied, if not they would be dissatisfied. This simple yet powerful idea offers two distinct ways to marketers how they can "influence" customer satisfaction. If firms want to raise the average satisfaction of customers, they could potentially raise the "received value" of the offer (e.g., through better quality, better service, etc.) or they could attempt to lower the prior expectations of customers. Of course, the second idea seems a little bit strange but, as we shall soon see, it is the preferred strategy of reverse psychology marketers.

In the context of traditional marketing, we often see the practice that companies, in an early stage of the life cycle, introduce products that have a less-than-acceptable level of value. This frequently happens in the consumer electronics and other high-tech categories. At that time, people usually have higher expectations than what they really get (see Figure 6.1). They would even be willing to pay a little bit more to have their expectations met. Over time, however, these expectations keep on increasing because of the communication of different companies promising additional features and because of learning and adaptation effects in the consumers themselves. The companies, as a consequence, feel the need to continuously augment the nature of their offerings. Their motivation,

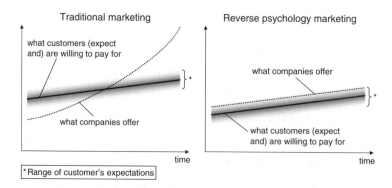

Figure 6.1 How reverse psychology manages expectations

as we have suggested, is to do better than the rivals in terms of product's features and functionalities. But to do this they often place undue emphasis on the product's features and less on the overall *value*. This usually results in a kind of over-marketing. Consumers find that the offerings in many categories do indeed top their expectations but they *far exceed what they are willing to pay for*. So, instead of being satisfied they find themselves in a situation that there are too many features and functions, all for additional costs that they cannot justify. So, prospective buyers do not buy and the company ends up with lower profits.

The reverse psychology marketers operate from an altogether different perspective. They play a well-honed strategy of "managing buyer expectations". The goal is always to keep these expectations very low and then attempt to do somewhat better so that people are left with a feeling of a pleasant surprise. The Lidls, Aldis, Wal-Marts, and Ryanairs communicate to the public that they can expect very little aside from the very functional aspect of the product and service they offer. Since low price is the principal motivator, customers expect to perform a number of services by themselves. So, people usually have very low expectations of these firms prior to purchase. Given this type of situation, such simple things as the smile on a sales agent or stewardess could be something that many people think that they had not bargained for and they are consequently happy with the whole experience. In Germany, the supermarket chain Aldi did not accept customers' bank debit cards for a long time. While other stores had made their usage routine, Aldi stood its ground firmly. Then, as the company branched into selling non-food items, its management realized that it made good business sense to allow the use of debit cards and they eventually did. For Aldi shoppers this was an added benefit to the already low prices, so they felt especially gratified. In different consumer surveys Aldi is rated as the food store with the most satisfied customers.

What are the macro reasons for these anti-marketing practices?

One could also explain the rise of these above trends and practices from a number of demand- and supply-related factors that are peculiar to the present time.

1. *Over-marketing*: This is the obvious culprit and has a number of different aspects. Those firms that have followed the usual marketing script have engaged in too many ads, too many product variations, outlets, channels, brand extensions, and so on. This inevitably has weakened brand image, confused buyers, and muddled their choice processes. In contrast, these new firms that are defying the rules of conventional marketing seem to engender a fresh level of curiosity, interest, support, and liking.

2. *Low marketing credibility*: People do not have a high degree of trust in what most traditional firms say and claim in their ads. There is an

ever-increasing sense of cynicism and frustration with businesses stemming from the pervasive belief that they are principally self-aggrandizing and profit-centered. Several recent high-profile corporate scandals in the U.S., Europe, and Japan have dented the image of large multinationals. All of these developments have contributed to a general mistrust about the marketing messages of firms. From this perspective, consumers view anti-marketing and its unpretentious and spin-free tactics as a much-needed and welcome change.

3. *Information overload*: As has been stated before, the overload of information is now higher than ever. In newspapers, magazines, on TV, on different websites, and also through other forms of communication, such as product placement in TV shows and films, the consumer is constantly told what product is good and which one he or she should buy. Companies are investing more and more money into their ad campaigns since they think that is the best way to reach more customers. A "marketing fog" type of situation has consequently developed, whereby all of these messages are getting lost in a hodge-podge of advertising claims and counter-claims. The net result is that people are effectively tuning off all commercials and becoming even less interested in the selling message. Instead, they are turning in large numbers to the Internet, which affords them the latitude and freedom to independently seek out information and compare shops on their own time and of their free will.

4. *Customer boredom*: One additional consumer-side reason is that people are generally fatigued and bored with all of the familiar traditional marketing ploys and gimmicks and are looking for new and creative approaches from marketers. From this perspective, the novel and counter-intuitive ploys that most anti-marketers apply have the capacity to intrigue, bemuse, and interest the buyer.

5. *Cost cutting*: Finally, the reason some firms are using anti-marketing tactics is very simple. They simply cannot afford the conventional approach. In several instances where the company has instituted new, reverse psychology tactics, it did so because it did not have sufficient money for a traditional branding campaign. Ironically, in the end, what was done to save costs became more effective. When Red Bull launched its energy drink for the European public, its managers wanted to use TV ads. But there was not enough money to pay for actors and crew. So, in their commercials they decided to use hand-drawn cartoons instead, which subsequently became part of the brand legend.

How can firms cope in this scenario?

The high level of success that anti-marketing and reverse psychology techniques have had has made firms of all sizes and functions sit up and take notice. They *too* want to think of ways they can co-opt some of these approaches in their own marketing. At the outset, it is a good idea to look at possible benchmarks and see if similar strategies are applicable for one's own brand or company. But, an obvious *caveat* is in order. To unabashedly copy the marketing tactics of another company is not really anti-marketing, and certainly not original marketing. The success of many of the past anti-marketing ploys was related to the product categories in which they were introduced. In fact, some of these ideas may be more conducive to symbolic, image-conscious categories like shops, restaurants, youth apparel, and high-end beverages. One may add that in equal or greater measure the effectiveness of some of these campaigns have drawn from the socially rebellious and quirky personalities of the entrepreneurs (like Richard Branson, Sam Walton, Michael O'Leary, and Nigo), who instituted them.

Nonetheless, it is clear that an increasing number of people would like to see firms not be so obvious in the selling message and to lighten up a little in their marketing. Sir Richard Branson, who earned his fame from founding and running the Virgin Atlantic airline, understood this popular yearning well. Virgin endeared itself to its audience from the playful and jocular humor in its ads. Its messages were invariably pro-consumer, placing itself as a champion of the masses, and incessantly poking fun at the established carriers. In fact, the lack of seriousness that Virgin portrayed about the entire airline business made its principal rival British Airways seem old-fashioned and stodgy. From that standpoint, Virgin and Sir Freddie Laker's People Express before it have ushered in the new and carefree age of travel, where fare is the best denominator and where people discount past concerns about trust and safety, and appear content to fly no-name, upstart carriers.

For each firm there should, however, be a way of finding one's own unique, suitable, and authentic anti-marketing approach. To bring this into effect, the company has to examine itself carefully and understand the true meaning of its mission and offering as understood by the buying public. The consumer is always ready for an honest, frank, and open dialogue with the seller. Information about products is invariably skewed in favor of firms. Some exploit it to their best financial advantage by encouraging consumers to buy more than what they need, using fear and ignorance as their allies. Therefore, any attempt to place the buyer on an even footing, albeit at a detriment to the selling process, will be viewed very positively and can eventually be rewarding. In the U.S., Progressive insurance company has launched an ad campaign in which it asks prospective buyers to compare its rates against those of its competitors. The firm says very clearly that its own quotes may not always be the best and that competitors may offer better rates in some cases. Buyers are encouraged to visit its website to make the rate comparison for themselves. This sort of message is very refreshing and clear to the average consumer. Obviously, it takes courage for managers to be truly honest with their customers and take a "come what may" philo-sophy. The examples cited above show that custom-ers are ready to meet a firm more-than-halfway if they see a genuine change in the firm's message and the actual way it does business.

7

Conclusions – The big picture

The recently deceased business and management thinker Peter Drucker once made a very insightful observation about marketing. He reflected that the true goal of marketing is to *obviate selling*. Marketing, in its ideal state, should fill a real human need and should then be able to execute its plan so seamlessly and effortlessly that no salesperson would ever need to come knocking on the doors. This idea is the same as the proverbial "selling like hot cakes". The baker does not need a bullhorn to call out for buyers and announce that the cakes are ready. If the latter are any good, buyers will dutifully appear on their own. Their fresh smell is the best advertising. It should be understood that the philosophy underlying reverse psychology marketing is exactly that. It should be possible to market a product or a service in such a natural and understated manner that customers don't feel they are being pressured to buy something. This is also reminiscent of Lao Tzu's famous Taoist dictum of *wu-wei* – "doing nothing and yet everything gets done".

We have discussed at length why such an approach has become desirable and necessary in our society at the present time. Marketing sadly has become equated with puffery and spin, as the art of circumlocution and perhaps even of deception. The textbooks of marketing actually recommend the practice of making "superiority claims" (like the "best", "fastest", "greatest", "ultimate", etc.) in ads because it is supposed to be the sure way to stand out and get noticed, and also to assist in a consumer's learning and recall. The consequence of this has been the veritable forest of extraordinary and vociferous claims from different sellers, all screaming to get attention and trial. Many therefore consider the phrase "high-pressure salesman" today as a tautology. Indeed, some of the "tactics" that push marketers employ, such as those annoying pop-up ads, direct marketing in people's homes, and the endless use of customer surveys, are seen by the average citizen as inescapable nuisances of a modern-day consumerist culture. But it did not have to come to this state. If people wanted to buy something, they would willingly seek out information about it and flock to the store on their own free will, without needing to be aggressively told what to do and reminded again and again. One is therefore heartened by the stories of people queuing up late in the night to acquire the latest Playstation, a *Harry Potter* book, or to get in first on an Ikea store opening.

Already, however, there are signs that change is on the way. It is becoming increasingly clear and obvious that many people have finally decided that they are not going to put up with the usual ways of marketers anymore. The practice of direct marketing, that is selling by calling people's homes at late hours, has been discussed and criticized by the U.S. Congress and there are laws in place about what marketers can or cannot do. More and more Americans are signing up to ensure not to be called at home, and many people are using pop-up blockers and digital video recorders (DVRs), which allow them to skip over TV commercials. But advertisers are finding new ways of getting around the available tools only to be able to *impose* their views on their hapless targets. It is becoming a custom to overtly "place" a product within the tableau of a film or television show allowing it to come in constant and direct view of the audience. The latest breed of pop-up ads is also able to bypass the blocking software that most people have on their computers. It is hence becoming a sorry sight that people and marketers are engaged in a desperate and costly struggle to stay one step ahead of each other, all to little avail.

The more hopeful signs are related to the ever-increasing use of the Internet among the populaces of the world. Internet is innately and essentially a "pull medium", despite the many fruitless efforts to turn it to push. Notwithstanding the omnipresent and always-annoying pop-up ads which most of us rush to delete, people surf the web on their own volition and under total control. As we have mentioned, the Google search engine has become a widespread success because it dutifully delivers what people ask of it, nothing more and nothing less. An increasing number of consumers are seeking out information about the brands they buy, being less impressed by the glitziness and glamour of the site but more by the concrete information and data it provides about the product. That brings us to the second aspect of the Internet. It actively calls for and even encourages a very *rational* form of processing. The large number of available "comparison sites" invoke the need to weigh and trade off the quality, features, and prices of different brands. Manufacturers are better off providing the relevant information about their products in an easily understood and straightforward manner and then letting the buyers arrive at their decisions by themselves. There is no need nor scope to pressure and stress the buyer by applying the usual "hard sell" techniques – in fact, the format of the Internet does not quite allow it. To that extent, the Tao of the Internet is very much suited to pull marketing.

In the rest of this chapter, we highlight the three key ideas of this book, the takeaways to consider and apply in one's own business, and discuss a little more about reverse psychology marketing and its process.

1. "Less is more"

This is one of the major themes of this book. An essential tendency for the practitioners of traditional marketing is to offer *more* to customers: more variety, more selection, more features, more stores, more brand extensions, more promotions, and so on. There is an underlying belief that more is somehow better, that customers thereby are better served, and the firm will benefit as a result. Generally speaking, most people view *some* choice as beneficial and good but the problem arises when it is carried, as has been, to an obvious excess. Over-marketing has become the norm for many businesses. There are far too many brand offerings within the same category, too many price tiers, too many stores, and too many confusing features. Managers have to understand the fact that there are diminishing returns from offering more, and at some point the results are bound to become negative. The overall brand mystique is going to suffer, which is a far more pernicious long-term damage. From this perspective, the recent decisions of DaimlerChrysler to offer a bewildering variety of different "classes" of Mercedes-Benz cars, such as the A, B, C, E, M, R, G, etc., have already confused many prospective buyers and have diluted the brand.

Offering less is a basic concept behind reverse psychology marketing. The idea is not just to convey scarcity but also to connote a certain value, mystique, and allure to the market. People are more intrigued these days with firms that do not fall into the usual pattern of over-reaching, over-publicity, and over-exposure. Porsche cars are so highly valued because they have managed, by and large, to hold their own in spite of the changing times. The look and feel of the Porsche 911 has not changed for more than a generation. There have been a few occasional feature additions, such as the incorporation of electronic technology, but the models have stayed the same. The same principle applies to authors, artists, musicians, and creators of all kinds. Lately, when a certain author writes a best-selling book, the immediate inclination is to publish a slew of follow-on titles all of incremental worth and questionable value. Invariably, however, it is the first book that really stands out. There is a feeling among the freshly minted successes to "cash in while the going is hot". Hence, the usual propensity among certain best-selling business authors to hit the global lecture circuit being introduced as some newly anointed management guru. While a few make a genuine contribution, most do not.

It is far better for firms and creators alike not to overreach themselves and to grow organically where possible. A truly great new idea for a book, music, or product is a rare event. The artists and authors whose work has endured the ages created their work through contemplation and assiduity that lasted many years. People are less impressed with firms and individuals who seek to draw attention to themselves with something that is obviously superficial and is designed to secure a pecuniary benefit. One respects more those so-called "quiet companies" that do their daily business, make hard-earned profits, and enrich their shareholders without a lot of flash and bravado. Likewise, there is a special charisma and mystique accorded to those individuals who have achieved success with their creations but who do not seek to bask in the limelight, and in fact stay away from it. The Japanese creator of the BAPE brand does not give out his real name calling himself self-effacingly as Nigo or number two, since, as per his logic, number one is a certain other Japanese celebrity who he is said to physically resemble. Mr Nigo actively shuns publicity and media interviews, limits the sales of his line, and still has a huge worldwide following. Likewise, the teenagers forming the rock phenomenon *Arctic Monkeys* have sought to keep a very low profile deflecting all of the media attention from themselves. They assert that it is their music that matters and what really speaks for them. In fact, they did something quite remarkable and unprecedented by turning down an invitation to appear at a major award-presentation event, something an expert publicist or marketing consultant would not recommend to a rock band at an early stage of their career. But their growing fan-base loves them even more *because* of it.

2. Need for "authenticity"

The second point of this book is that the true purpose underlying all reverse psychology marketing is to make a firm and its products look more honest and genuine with the customers. That is its *one and only* goal. The success of any of these above-discussed ploys is incumbent on the extent to which a business or individual is able to accomplish that effectively.

But to do that with a measure of conviction and credibility there must really *be* something honest and genuine about the business itself, its message, and its method. Managers should therefore be ready to account for any failings and shortcomings of their products, and of past management, marketing, and advertising practices. They should adopt the attitude of "back to first principles" by aligning themselves, their employees, and business styles with their core missions and the needs of all stakeholders, including the broader community. With growing public sentiments in favor of conservation, ecological balance, and good corporate citizenship, there is now a higher calling and firms and their executives are not exempt from answering to that.

There is at present a worldwide outcry for things that are natural and genuine, and not fake and contrived. This development really extends *beyond* the popularity of organic, non-GM foods in supermarkets. The public now wants products that have been "honestly made" by manufacturers who have paid a fair, living wage to their workers in the less-developed countries. In addition, they expect that these firms, in their cost-cutting approaches, have not made compromises with anything that endangers public health, the environment, and the ecology. Companies all over the world are waking up to this reality every day. As a result, more and more firms are joining the "social responsibility bandwagon" and the championing the well-known causes of the day. The coffee-store chain Starbucks assures its customers that it sources its coffee beans only from those suppliers that pay an honest wage to the small farmers and who also help build their communities. The big oil companies like Shell and BP have, in their marketing, reinforced their commitment to the environment and the research for renewable energy sources. Philip Morris, the cigarette giant and the maker of *Marlboro*, runs very graphic commercials on American television, pointedly asking young people not to smoke. This counter-intuitive campaign strikes some people as being rather odd but the company is merely reacting to the pressures (and the risks of potential litigation) of the time.

Even the people managing and appearing in various broadcasting and media channels are feeling the same pinch to forgo the usual marketing techniques of the past in favor of approaches that are more genuine and authentic. Newspaper and magazine editors, radio and television producers, anchors, columnists, and writers have seen a recent backlash against their usual glib and "packaged" tactics that they used to cater to their audiences. They understand that the public mood has suddenly shifted. There is now a growing popular sentiment that the media is too marketing-oriented, too spin-prone, too focused on political correctness and on toeing the party line. Hence, a fresh crop of newspaper columnists, television and radio personalities who speak their mind without fear or inhibition, even at the risk of offending or causing offense, are gaining particular favor and popularity. In America, talk show host Bill O'Reilly of

Fox News has garnered a rabid, cult-like following by espousing various right-wing causes and by unabashedly castigating the liberal mindset. His show is labeled as the "no spin zone" with the stock slogan: "The spin stops here." Simon Cowell, one of the judges appearing on the hit talent search programme *American Idol*, seems to have made rudeness a virtue (and a popularity ploy) by appearing caustic and scathing towards the less-gifted contestants. He has become infamous for his acerbic put-downers that reduce a few to tears. Yet, he is a favorite of the masses because he is seen as an authentic person and not concealing his views in polite, saccharine-sweet, and euphemistic terms. Even Donald Trump and his somewhat self-important persona that are on view in *The Apprentice* show appeal to a lot of viewers. Many respect his achievements and understand that his egotism *is* his authentic self and is an essential concomitant of his success.

Therefore, in the end, the common and overwhelming theme that runs across nearly all reverse psychology methods is genuineness and the lack of pretense. At a time when spin has entered the popular lexicon, as a label for all that is wrong about marketing and business, being honest and open has become the essential virtue. The following story illustrates this appeal in a particularly apt way. A letter recently written by a fund manager of Legg Mason, a brokerage firm, to the investors caught the attention of the world press. In it, Bill Miller, who manages the $20 billion Value Trust fund, writes,

You are probably aware that the Legg Mason Value Trust has outperformed the S&P 500 index for each of the past 15 calendar years. That may be the reason you decide to purchase the fund. If so, we are flattered but believe you are setting yourself up for a disappointment... *our so-called "streak" is a fortunate accident of the calendar... If your expectation is that we will outperform the market every year, you can expect to be disappointed* (italics added).

In our view, this is the best kind of reverse psychology.

3. The power of the network

Finally, at every stage this book has emphasized that in today's markets seeding, building, and then sustaining a network of customers is vitally important for every business. The success or failure of any firm and its products is inextricably linked to the size, loyalty, and buying behavior of the corresponding buyer network. If one considers how certain brands have achieved cult status and became worldwide phenomena, one can always find a dedicated base that rallied in support of these brands, spread positive word-of-mouth to others, and made the critical difference. For even a reasonably successful product, it is always possible to find a small group of loyal buyers that constitute the core part of the network, the ones who buy often and show less sensitivity to price variations. In fact, the Pareto principle (80:20 rule) can be said to operate for many businesses, which means that a relatively minor fraction of the customer population contribute a disproportionate amount of the firm's revenues. The rest of the buyers are the so-called "switchers", who show less loyalty, have an innate mercenary motive, and are ready to defect to a lower-priced (or better-value) offering at the first opportunity. It is obviously imperative for every firm that its managers make an effort to understand the psychology of the core loyal group and attempt to please them above all others.

From this perspective, the customer satisfaction metrics that many firms use to gauge the effectiveness of their marketing strategies often prove to be a mirage. There have been several instances of companies that have attained high customer satisfaction scores but still seen customers defect on a regular basis. The reason that these metrics do not offer a truer picture is that they do not account for the underlying heterogeneity of the customer base. At any given point of time, the switchers may be satisfied with the firm and its products, claim themselves to be very satisfied, and then leave at the sight of a better deal. The opinions of the "loyals" are relatively more stable and reliable. Thus, if the firm were to use customer satisfaction as a performance measure, it would find itself aiming at a continuously moving target. The marketplace dynamics depending on the mix between switchers and loyals, their behavioral differences, and the actions of competing firms incessantly work on changing the satisfaction of the customer base. It should therefore be understood that customer satisfaction is not a goal or a "fixed target". It is at best a fleeting image and a momentary snapshot of the market's mood. To get a better understanding of the strength of the network, it is far more helpful to investigate the loyal customers in greater depth.

As a general rule, businesses today should focus more on the art of pulling customers than on pushing their products and viewpoints on them. If the firm is able to articulate its product and brand philosophy clearly, make intelligent use of ambassadors or network hubs, and use publicity or buzz as invaluable allies the brand network will grow on its own merits. And the "pulled customer" is a *better* customer. He or she is more motivated because he has come on his own accord. He may have done the prior research on the Internet, so he needs less persuasion in the store or showroom. Such a customer costs less to sell and service, can attract others without much influence, and can stay with the firm for a very long time. By taking that perspective, marketing can then be said to have fulfilled its intrinsic mission – the Druckerian ideal to obviate selling.

The reverse psychology marketing process

The trends towards the adoption, application, and practice of reverse psychology tactics by firms are taking place across many industries and many countries. These are presently more concentrated in the consumer goods categories, especially those where buyer involvement and purchase stake are high as is the case for luxury products. This is so because the notions underlying reverse psychology add that key element of cachet and allure to the luxury products and people find it important to show off to others the exclusivity of the brands they own. In contrast, the use of reverse psychology is less developed in instances where the buyer is motivated not so much by prestige and symbolism but more by the functional nature of the product, and the buying process is more mechanical and formalized as in the business-to-business arena. However, when one considers that the major aspects of this philosophy entail such ideas as adopting an understated approach ("less is more"), being more authentic, and paying greater attention to the customer network, it is clear that the concepts and techniques of reverse psychology are equally pertinent to *all* businesses.

There is a very interesting, but much less publicized, dimension to the question: "Why is there a need for reverse psychology marketing today?" Its answer can be found in the "untold" history of the role of marketing in firms and the consequent maturation of the consumer. Note that in this book we have used the term "push marketing" to denote the practice, very common in these and earlier times, whereby a marketer attempts to foist a product or a message on the reluctant and hapless public. Traditionally, marketing has seen its mission as being derived from the firm's objective of catering to the needs of its customers. From a practical standpoint, however, businesses quickly understood that people's needs were only so many and that to continue to grow and prosper they would have to somehow "create needs and multiply wants". People had to be told, retold, and, in fact, "educated" that they really and absolutely needed to buy something. Otherwise, their lives would be unglamorous and incomplete, and society and convention would not accept them as fully functional members. So, it fell to marketing to devise ways by which these ideas and views were ingrained in people's minds. This ushered in the "era of push" and firms sought relentlessly to make the public aware of a specific need or want that they had not felt and known before. Thus, everyone had to get a certain high-tech gadget. Women were told that they needed more than one type of cream for their body and face; they had to get one sort for the day and another for the night. People were informed that their balding pates, slowing libidos, and "restless legs" were undesirable medical conditions that could, and must, be redressed. And so on. It is perhaps up to an anthropologist or a sociologist to decide how many of these "needs" were genuine and worthwhile, and where business and marketing truly made a difference. Figure 7.1 shows the process by which the present ideas of reverse psychology marketing have evolved.

As businesses delivered on meeting the wants that they had created, a gap soon developed between supply and demand. Some cannier consumers refused

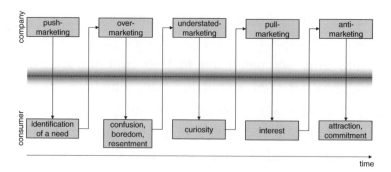

Figure 7.1   Reverse psychology marketing process

to be swayed by the firms' messages and remained
stuck to their positions of not falling in with the rest
of the public. It became clear that the mechanism
of push marketing could not work on these people
and at all times. That, in turn, led to the practice
of over-marketing that one frequently sees today. Its
ultimate goal is to persuade, cajole, and convince
the people who are still sitting on the fence to join
in with the buying public. But, that strategy has so
far failed and many brands have been damaged as a
result. Indeed, as has been already mentioned, over-
marketing comes with the usual consequences, of
which buyer boredom, confusion, and resentment are
only a few. Next, the savvier business players devised
a different strategy – an understated marketing tone
that was so different from the usual aggressive kind
that it genuinely evoked customer curiosity. People
began to feel that something new and different was
in the air. What is happening presently is that the
more shrewd and nimble firms have branched into
advanced pull marketing and anti-marketing techniques that are better able to interest, engage, and
captivate the buyers and keep them for life.

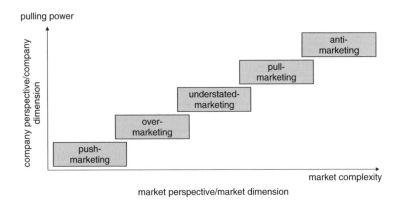

Figure 7.2 Stages in the evolution of reverse psychology marketing

Figure 7.2 shows the same concept but from a different perspective. The various types of marketing, as discussed above, are illustrated as stages in a process of progression. The development from push marketing to anti-marketing is represented as an evolution of marketing strategies and practices over time. Note that this view is not just limited to the company perspective but really extends beyond it. If one considers the general market condition and thinks of the different kinds of tactics used by firms and the reactions they draw from consumers, one gets a very similar picture. As the market has become increasingly more complex and the consumers savvier and more blasé as a result, more sophisticated approaches are now necessary to win their favors. The resulting firm strategy can be based on understated marketing, pull marketing, or anti-marketing, all of which employ reverse psychology in one form or another and have progressively greater gravitational power on the public.

Some final thoughts

There is one essential truth about marketing that escapes many people, including many of its scholars and experts. *Marketing is very much an art and far less a science.* The vast number of contemporary textbooks, theories, and "paradigms" seem to accord undue weight to the latter while tending to undermine the former. Every concept or notion in marketing is usually simplified to a causal process, in a building block or equation form, which leaves little room for the ways in which the buyers *actually* think and act. Perhaps, those humble, battle-hardened sellers who practice it daily in the streets, shops, and bazaars around the world understand the craft better. They know that to practice marketing well in the field setting, one must employ an element of wizardry that derives not so much from rational logic but from sheer perspicacity, creativity, opportunism, and genius. Here, understanding the mindset of individual buyers and their decision-making "levers" is the key. The good sellers quickly realize that to carry out their trade they must perforce combine the skills of a psychologist with a measure of artistry and magic.

That there is an element of instinctive acumen and wizardry in good marketing is beyond dispute. Just like a professional conjurer pulls a rabbit out of an empty hat, a clever marketer is able to create something out of a seeming nothing. On a slow sales day, an ice-cream seller gives away free ice-cream to a few children and has them do a walk-about in the immediate vicinity of the store. Soon, the delectable sight of the melting cones is enough to awaken the taste buds of more than few passers-by and business picks up once again. The American bookseller Barnes & Noble similarly understands that allowing shoppers to read the books from its shelves freely, without restriction, and even while they are drinking coffee, actually *increases* sales. At these stores one frequently sees some people taking copious notes from textbooks and travel-guides that they presumably would not buy. Any rational observer would think it a counterproductive business practice to allow potential book buyers read without paying; and then permit food and drinks to come in close proximity of the new and unsold books! Nonetheless, the admirable aspect to this tactic is that it works. Stores like Barnes & Noble act as magnets for bibliophiles the world over. They come each week in large numbers, lounge on comfortable sofas, munch on cakes and brownies, and spend long hours leafing through all kinds of books. And they *do* buy, taking home more than a few and keeping the cash registers constantly busy.

The story is also told that the redoubtable Mrs Esther Lauder got her break in the highly competitive world of cosmetics and perfumes through a lucky "accident". She had fortuitously spilled her new Youth Dew line on the carpets of the Paris department store Galeries Lafayette. The pungent fragrance attracted a crowd of curious shoppers and Youth Dew subsequently made the name and fortune of the fledgling

Estée Lauder label. Similarly, most music buffs and raconteurs attribute the early success of the Beatles to the marketing genius of their manager Brian Epstein. He is credited with not only "cleaning up" their act by making them wears suits and give up swearing in public. A lesser-known fact is that he actually paid a few young Liverpool girls to shriek as soon the group would appear on stage. The phenomenon caught on and the Beatles were forever associated with shrieking adolescent girls.

In recent years there has been far too much emphasis placed in the academic and corporate worlds on the "science of marketing". It is based on the dubious logic that marketing can be quantified and as the saying goes "that which cannot be measured, cannot be managed". Academicians never seem to tire of the prospect of "modeling marketing" by bringing in sophisticated statistical, econometric, and game-theory formulations to arrive at usually prosaic "X causes Y" sorts of insights. Their conclusions would fail to impress any semiliterate but reasonably competent Third World shopkeeper, who has a far better inkling of the factors that make people buy. Corporate marketing managers, on the other hand, often spend vast sums of money into pointless marketing campaigns and exercises. In their scheme too, everything has to be reduced to numbers, which should help in keeping track of the return on their investments and measure the performance of their underlings. But, as we have stated, the result of all of this has been the expensive and fruitless practice of over-selling. A more regrettable fall-out is that by following this line of thinking one has missed out on the subtlety and the key essence of marketing. This book has pointed to a few ways by which the "lost magic" of marketing can be regained and its primacy established in the mindsets of its votaries.

In the end that should be the starting point.

Finis

Index